Trading खाता

OrangeBooks Publication

Smriti Nagar, Bhilai, Chhattisgarh - 490020

Website: **www.orangebooks.in**

© Copyright, 2022, Author

All rights reserved. No part of this book may be reproduced, stored in a retrieval system, or transmitted, in any form by any means, electronic, mechanical, magnetic, optical, chemical, manual, photocopying, recording or otherwise, without the prior written consent of its writer.

First Edition, 2022

TRADING
खाता

A BEGINNERS GUIDE TO THE STOCK MARKET

ANIKET KUMAR PATEL

OrangeBooks Publication
www.orangebooks.in

Disclamer

The Book is for educational purpose only and should not be considered as an advice of any nature. Nothing in this book is for trading or investment advice. The sole purpose of this book is to give some educational contain to the readers also all views and thoughts shared in this book are authors personal views and opinion. You should not rely on any statement made by author in this book for investment or trading in any instrument. Do consult your financial advisor or use our own setup before trading. Neither the Author nor publisher will be responsible for profit or loss made by you. Information given in this book should not be regarded as a complete analysis of the subject discussed in this book. You are advised to do forward and back test of strategies discussed in this book also taking advice of authorized financial advisor/consultant is must. All advices and strategies have potential of profit and loss. You will be solely responsible for the decision made by you after reading this book. All expressions of the opinion reflect the sole judgment of the author as on the date of publication and are subject to change. The publisher and author accept no liability of profit/loss or damage of any kind that may result from you're trading or investing. Trading or investments are subject to market risk. Do consult your financial advisor before taking any trade.

Index

1. A Brief History Of Indian Stock Market 1
2. Market Participants 5
3. NSE (National Stock Exchange) 8
4. SEBI (Stock Exchange Board Of India) 11
5. Important Terminologies Of Stock Market 13
6. Focus, Discipline, Practice And Patience Needed For Learning 17
7. People's Perceptions And Misunderstanding About Trading And Stock Market 19
8. Common Mistakes Beginners Do In Trading 20
9. My Trading Rules (A Chapter Of Risk Management) 23
10. Analyzing Candle- Stick Chart 25
11. How To Trade A Candle 28
12. How To Draw Trend Line 55
13. Understanding Price Patterns 57
14. Various Types Of Price Patterns 58
15. How To Identify Right Brake Out 72
16. Fear & Greed 73
17. Learn And Earn With Market's Move 74
18. Who Is The Boss? 76
19. Trading Journal 100 Day's Trading Challenge To Improve Our Trading 77

Trading खाता

A Brief History Of Indian Stock Market

The story of Indian stock market started under a banyan tree.

Yes under a banyan tree in 1850's, one day four Guajarati and a Parsi man meets under a banyan tree in front of Mumbai town hall the purpose was to do informal trade of cotton. They did not know the activities done by them would bring a huge change in the future of people and Indian economy.

Gradually the group grew and later on they formed an association called "The native share and stock broker's association."

The Bullion King

Premchand Roychand, one of the most influential businessmen of 19th century Bombay. A man who created a fortune in the stocks brokering business and became famous as cotton king. Also known with the names The Bullion king or Big Bull and he were the founder of the native share and stock broker's.

It was the year of 1875 in which the first official stock exchange renamed as "Bombay stock exchange" came in existence.

There are many stock brokering companies in Mumbai that have been around since the time the stock market was formally launched in India.

In 1894 the Ahmadabad Stock Exchange came into existence, which mainly dealt in the shares of textile mills. The Calcutta stock exchange was started in 1908 to provide a market for shares of plantation and jute mills. Than in 1920 the Madras stock exchange came in existence.

The Indian stock market has seen many Up's and Down's in more than 150 year's.

At present there are 24 stock exchanges in India in which 21 are regional ones with allotments of two each are setup by reform. National stock exchange (NSE) and Over the Counter Exchange of India (OTCEI) have mandate of nationwide Trading.

"SENSEX"

On 2nd January 1986 BSE developed an index named SENSEX to measure the performance of exchange. In 1990 SENSEX closed above 1000. In 1992 it touched another milestone of 4000. Than 1st may 1992 government come up with SEBI Act to protect, develop and regulate the securities market. Also Security Appellate Tribunal established in same year.

"BSE On-Line Trading (BOLT) System"

An open outcry flour trading exchange switched to electronic system developed by CMC ltd. BOLT expanded nationwide in 1997 with the capacity of 8 million orders per day.

In 1921 Bank of India started acting as a clearing house. Later on In 1957 BSE granted permanent recognition under Securities Contracts (Regulation) Act (SCRA). BSE moved to the Phiroze Jeejeebhoy Towers at Dalal Street, Fort area.

Indian Stock market came in mass participation from the general public when Mr.Dhirubhai Ambani came up with Reliance IPO in 1980.

BSE is Asia's oldest stock exchange. It is the world's 7th largest stock exchange with an overall market capitalization of more than **US$2.8 trillion** on as of February 2021.

Other important events

9th June 2000	**Equity derivatives introduced**
1st June 2001	**Index options launched**
9th July 2001	**Stock options launched**
1st Nov 2001	**Stock futures launched**
19th Aug 2005	**BSE become cooperate entity**
1st Oct 2008	**Currency derivatives introduced**
18th May 2009	**The S&P BSE SENSEX raised 2110.70 points (17.34%) and Index-wide upper circuit breaker applied**
21st Sep 2010	**First to introduce Mobile-based Trading**
1st Oct 2018	**BSE launches its commodity derivatives segment making it India's 1st Universal Exchange**

Market Participants

Those whom so ever are participating in market directly or indirectly are known as market participants. It may be an individual or organization we can classify them in following category:

1. Retail Traders Or Investors
2. NRI's or OCI's
3. Domestic Institutional Investors
4. Assets Management Companies
5. Foreign Institutional Investors
6. Regulatory Authorities
7. Financial Institutions And Banks
8. Stock Brokers
9. Clearing Co-Operations
10. Stock Exchanges

Now will discuss in detail about every participants

1. **Retail Traders Or Investors** - these are small players like me and you in terms of capital. 4.7% are retail traders in Indian stock market and some data confirms the grim truth that 70-80% of retail traders are unprofitable.

2. **NRI's or OCI's** – these are Indian origin people living outside India. Participating in stock market.

3. **Domestic Institutional Investors** – they are based in India undertaking investments in securities and other financial assets. They use pooled funds to trade in market and yes they affect the net investment flows into the economy.

4. **Assets Management Companies** - assets management companies are those companies who firm stake money from small investors to big and attempts to invest in securities.

5. **Foreign Institutional Investors** - these are the foreign institutions investing in Indian stock market have been one of the biggest drivers of India's financial market having invested more than 4000 cr. In 2021-22.

6. **Regulatory Authorities** - these are government or semi-government bodies established either by the act of parliament or general legislation. Their main function is to regulate market. Ex- SEBI, CDSL, NSDL etc.

7. **Financial Institutions And Banks** – financial institutions and bank plays important role in security market. They help in transferring money from bank account to trading account.

8. **Stock Brokers** – these are trading members of exchange. One cannot directly buy or sell security in stock exchanges without stocks brokers.

9. **Clearing Cooperation's** – the main function of clearing co-operations is to identify buyers and sellers matching debit and credit by doing this they ensure no default smooth running of clearance. Ex- NSCCL, ICCL

10. **Stock Exchanges** – they permit healthy speculation of securities and ensure demand And supply of securities and liquidity. NSE and BSE are main stock exchanges in India.

NSE (National Stock Exchange)

NSE is the largest financial exchange in Indian stock market.

Established in – 1992

Headquarter - Mumbai

It was established by government of India to provide solutions to simplify participation in stock market. And to make it more accessible to all market participants.

Functions

- Provide automated trading facility accross nation.
- Act as a communication network among investors and traders.
- Listing of IPO's, offers clearing and settlement services.
- Meet global standards for financial exchange market.
- Offers trading and investment in various financial products.

"Nifty 50"

In 1996 NSE launched S&P CNX Nifty (commonly known as Nifty 50) index. It's a benchmark index of NSE composed of top 50 traded stocks in its platform. It signifies the weighted average of top 50 trading stocks from 24 different sectors.

Nifty 50 Companies

1.	Reliance Industries	26.	Oil&Natural Gas Corporation
2.	TCS	27	Adani Ports & Special Economic Zones
3.	HDFC Bank	28.	Tech Mahindra
4.	Infosys	29.	HDFC Life Insurance Company
5.	Hindustan Unilever	30.	Divi's Laboratories
6.	HDFC	31.	Power Grid Corporation Of India
7.	ICICI Bank	32.	SBI Life Insurance Company
8.	Bajaj Finance	33.	NTPC
9.	State Bank Of India	34.	Bajaj Auto
10.	Wipro	35.	Bharat Petroleum Corporation
11.	Bharti Airtel	36.	Tata Motors

12.	Kotak Mahindra Bank	37.	.Indian Oil Corporation
13.	HCL Technology	38.	Grasim Industry
14.	Asian Paints	39.	Shree Cement
15.	Bajaj Fin Services	40.	Hindalco Industry
16.	ITC	41.	Mahindra&Mahindra
17.	Axis Bank	42.	Britannia Industries
18.	Larsen & Toubro	43.	Coal India
19.	Ultra Tech Cement	44.	Indusind Bank
20	Maruti Suzuki India	45.	Tata Consumer Products
21.	Nestle India	46.	Dr.Reddy's Laboratories
22.	Sun Pharmaceutical Industries	47.	Cipla
23.	Tata Steel	48.	Eicher Motors
24.	JSW Steel	49.	UPL
25.	Titan Company	50.	Hero Moto-Corp

SEBI (Stock Exchange Board Of India)

Established on – 12th April 1992

By an act of parliament- Security exchange board of India act 1992.

Head Office- Mumbai

Management Board of SEBI Consists of:

- Chairman
- 2 members from central government.
- 5 other members appointed by central government.
- 1 member from RBI.

Thus SEBI is a 9 Member body Including Chairman.

Following Are the Functions Of SEBI

1. Protection of the interests of investors in securities market.

2. Promotion and Development of Securities market in India.

3. Regulation of Stock exchanges and other security market in India.

4. To register and regulate the working of stock brokers, sub-brokers, portfolio managers, advisors and other intermediaries who may be associated with the security market.

5. Register various organizations and institutions.

6. Register and regulate funds and schemes.

7. Promote and regulate self regulatory organizations.

8. Prohibit fraudulent and unfair trade practices.

9. Promote investors 'education and training.

10. Prohibit insider trading in securities.

11. Regulate substantial acquisition of shares and takeover of companies.

12. conducting research for efficient working and development of securities market.

Important Terminologies Of Stock Market

1. **Share Or Stock** – a share is a part of company when a person buy share he/she becomes shareholder of a particular company. Whereas Stock is a collection of shares.

2. **Intraday Trading/Day Trading-** intraday is a practice of buying or selling shares of a company in same day.

3. **Buying/Long Position** – when a trader predicts price rise of a particular stock. He/she takes long position in that condition.

4. **Selling/Short Position** – when a trader predicts price fall of a particular stock. He/she takes short position in that condition.

5. **Short Covering-** short covering is closing a short position. In this condition first we have to buy same quantities of shares that have been shorted earlier.

6. **Bid Price-** it is the highest price at which a buyer is willing to pay to purchase stocks.

7. **Ask price-** it is also known as offer price at this price seller is willing to sell a particular share.

8. **Bid-Ask Spread** – it is the difference between bid prices and ask price.

9. **Target Price-** a target price is the price decided by the trader at which he has to book profit.

10. **Bullish-** if you are assuming the stock price rises will make higher highs than in that condition you are bullish on particular stock.

11. **Bearish-** if you are assuming that the stock price will fall.

12. **Limit Order-** in this order type a trader has to place limit buying or selling price before entering in a trade.

13. **Market Order-** in this order type trader place order at market price.

14. **Stop Loss-** this feature help trader to stop loss at certain price.

15. **Cover Order-** this feature help trader to put stop loss along with buying or selling order in intraday position.

16. **Bracket Order-** in this order type trader gets facility of placing target, stop loss along with limit buying or selling price.

17. **After Market Order-** this order type facilitates trader to place order before market opening.

18. **Upper Circuit-** it is the upper limit of share price. Decided by exchange.

19. **Lower Circuit** – it is the lowest limit of share price. Decided by the exchange.

20. **Volatility-** in stock market volatility refers to the fluctuation in the price of stock. If share price is moving steadily than it is considered as less volatile market where as if fluctuation is high than market is consider volatile.

21. **Liquidity-** liquidity depends upon share volume trading in exchange.

22. **Support Level** – it is the point from where stock price taking support in other words it is the price where demand of share is strong which prevent it from falling more.

23. **Resistance Level** – it is the point from where share price is facing rejection in other words it is the price where supply is strong which prevent it from raising more.

24. **Leverage-** also known as double edge sword. Leverage means borrowing money to trade in more quantities.

25. **OHLC-** it refers to Open, High, Low, Close

26. **Gap Up-** when share price open at higher rate than previous day closing price it is called gap up opening.

27. **Gap Down** – when share price open at low rate than previous day closing price it is called gap down opening.

28. **Market Trend-** it refers to a trend or continuation in price rise or price fall of share over a particular time period.

29. **Trend line-** trend lines are use to draw support and resistance. We connect two or more resistance or support points to draw trend line.

30. **Bull Market/Bear Market** – when market is dominated by buyers it is called bull market. Similarly when market is dominated by sellers than it is considered as bear market.

Focus, Discipline, Practice And Patience Needed For Learning

These three qualities are most important for a trader to build in our self. Focus on what you decided to do, discipline is what you decided one should stuck with it completely and practice these Do's and Don'ts because perfection comes with practice only. No one has these qualities by birth.

In trading management of emotions plays important role just because markets don't care about your emotion you have to work according to our rules, strategies and setup. While trading in a market one should know where to use which emotion. Many people say it's a game of greed and fear. So if you became master in managing our greed and fear you can flow with markets move.

Some habits which increase focus and help to increase concentration:

- **Eating healthy food.**
- **Doing physical exercise and yoga daily.**
- **Taking good sleep.**

- **Avoiding negative thoughts and negative people who have false knowledge about trading.**
- **Stop over thinking.**
- **Building logical thinking skill.**

People's Perceptions And Misunderstanding About Trading And Stock Market

Trading Is Gambling
No trading is not gambling, you will understand this concept only when you will first learn trading and then trade. What most of the beginners do?

They start trading before learning anything; I have meet many people who even don't know how to put stop- loss. They directly jumped into intraday trading just because there emotion says to do it or they got some tips through fraudulent.

Prediction Or Probability
There is lot of difference between prediction and probability. In prediction our emotions are involved. But probability is completely a different technical thing. In which logic, reasoning and calculation involved.

Common Mistakes Beginners Do In Trading

Borrow Money For Trading
Never borrow money for trading or investment it is not you asset it's a liability which you have to re-pay with interest. And no one in this market can give fixed return. Trading or investments are subject to market risk.

Trading on the basis of tips or calls.

Do our own analysis before taking a trade it's your money tip sellers or call providers don't care about it. Learn basic concepts of trading technical and fundamental analysis.

Emotional Trading
Where ever money plays a role it brings various emotions. Some time these emotions are good some time they are bad enough to wipes out our entire capital. Thus identification of emotion and emotional management plays important role in Trading.

Revenge Trading
Most of the time what trader do when their 1-2 stop- loss hit they get accustomed to their emotions and then they start placing trades on the basis of their emotions, keeping technical analysis aside.

Trading Without Stop-Loss
Common mistake beginners do. Not placing stop-loss either they don't know where to place stop-loss or due to over confidence.

Margin Trading
Margin trading is a tool of profit making for Pro-Traders not for beginners just because it increases risk and reward.

Trading Without Risk Management
If you will treat trading as a business and not as a speculation, then you will understand the concept of risk management very well and you will be able to apply it too. (Risk management will be explained in coming chapters).

Do Read Books, Watch News And Analyze Charts
If you consider trading as a business then it is very important for you to be alert in your trading and for alertness you need to read books, Analyze news and charts and then make an informed decision.

Do Trade Review

It is very important for a trader to review his trades because by reviewing we realize our mistakes, then where there is a possibility of improvement, it can be improved and where it shows the change, we can change it.

My Trading Rules (A Chapter Of Risk Management)

- Stock selection before next day market opening.
- News analysis of stocks selected.
- Chart analysis of stocks selected.
- Keeping a rough idea of entry, stop-loss and exit price.
- Evaluating our trading setup with market's mood.
- Analyzing pre-market.
- Avoiding over gap up and gap down openings.
- Taking trade only at price decided. Avoiding sudden price hikes.
- Putting stop-loss in each trade and trailing stop-loss when needed.
- Risk management through quantity control. Not on the basis of stop-loss.
- Taking as much risk as is affordable. Never take unaffordable risk.

- While analyzing stocks or taking trade always keeping two things in mind.
- No Emotion No opinion.
- Always hold profitable trades never hold loss- making trades.
- Trailing stop-loss after 1:2 risk rewards.
- Avoiding setup having less than 1:2 risk rewards.
- Never do over trading. Only trade in stocks or derivative analyzed in home work a day before.
- A trader should not re-invest the return or profit earned by him at the same rate of risk he has earned.
- Always keep our trading and personnel life separate.
- Never be over-motivated or de-motivated by looking at others. Always assess yourself. Put yourself in sculpting and not looking at others.
- All rules are subject to change according to markets need profit is ultimate motive.

10

Analyzing Candle-Stick Chart

So before we learn how to chart first it become necessary to know why it is important for a trader to analyze a chart

- Charts tell us history of stock.
- The chart shows us price movement.
- Charts show us the basic outlook of the risk associated with the price movement.

In this way charts help a trader to analyze stock. Well I prefer popularly used candle-stick chart for stocks analyses. In candle stick charts price movement is described with the help of candle stick.

What does the candle tells us?

Candle tells us the open, high, low and close of the price at a given point of time.

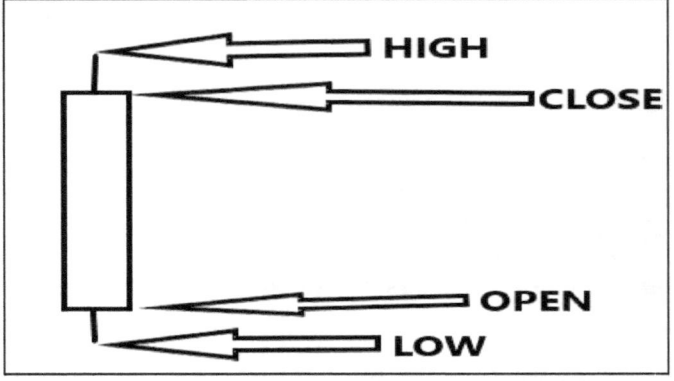

Open

Open is the first traded price of a stock in a given point of time. If price raises the candle start growing upward. Candle starts growing downward when price falls.

Low

Low is the least price traded in a given point of time. It is represented by the bottom edge of lower shadow. If there is an absence of lower shadow in that case low is equal to open price.

High

High is the highest price traded in a given point of time. It is represented by the top edge of upper shadow. If there is an absence of upper shadow in that case high is equal to the open price.

Close

It is the last traded price of stock in a given point of time. The determination of candle color (Red or Green) determined by the close. If candle closes above open price than it will be green otherwise red.

Range
Range is the difference between high and low in a particular interval of time.

Body
If price closes above open than it will form green candle otherwise red and this red and green color of candle shows the body of candle.

Shadow
The thin lines above or below candle body is known as shadow, wick or tail of a candle. Testing of price range is done by shadow where as we got confirmation through body.

Time Frame
There are various time frame used to analyze candle stick chart ex. 5 min, 15 min, day, weekly.

How To Trade A Candle

As discussed earlier candle shows us movement of price in a given point of time. There are various types of candles having our own characteristics meaning and logic.

- Hammer
- Inverted hammer
- Shooting star
- Morning star
- Evening star
- Hanging man
- Doji
- Bullish Engulf
- Bearish Engulf
- Bullish or bearish Harami
- Dark cloud cover
- Piercing line
- Belt hold
- Three black crown
- Three white soldiers

Will discuss all these candle sticks in detail. So before going through it let me clear one thing that even candlesticks fail too. There is nothing like 100% correct.

Hammer candle

✓ As you can see in the image it looks like hammer. Its upper wick is very small some time negligible and its lower wick is large with small body size at upper edge.

What does hammer interprets?

A candle tells us few things by its appearance:

✓ The long lower wick tells us the movement of price that the price fell to a support level than due to high buying pressure or seller's absence price bounced back to the open price.

✓ The absence of upper wick tells us that price never went more than opening price at given point of time.

✓ The body at upper side or the price closed at or near to open implies that the bulls overpowered bears.

✓ Thus the occurrence of Hammer at the bottom of down trend is clear indication of trend reversal.

(Note- if candle of same shape occur in uptrend than it's not a hammer it's a hanging man)

How To Trade Hammer Candle

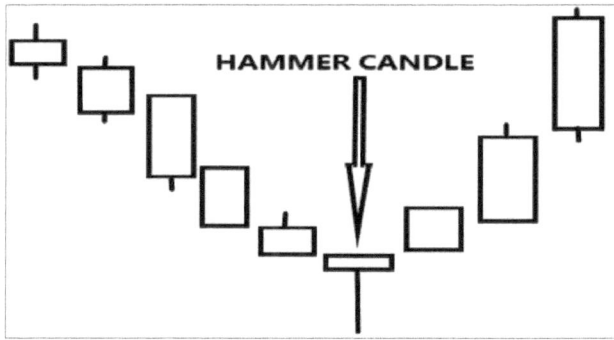

Some important points to be note down before entering in a Hammer candle trade.

- ✓ Formation of hammer candle at the down trend is the indication of trend reversal.
- ✓ Entry after confirmation candle is considered safer entry.
- ✓ One can enter after the close of hammer putting stop-loss at rejection point (bottom of lower tail from where price bounced back).
- ✓ If lower tail is much long creating a big stop-loss price than we can put SL at half of the lower tail.
- ✓ Longer the lower wick higher will be the bullish reversal.
- ✓ Next candle open above previous close with high volume is good confirmation.
- ✓ The target should be decided on the basis of previous resistance.
- ✓ Green hammer is much stronger than red.

Inverted Hammer Candle

As you can see in the image inverted hammer looks like hammer but in inverted form. It has big upper wick with negligible lower wick and small body at down side.

What does inverted hammer interprets?

A candle tells us few things by its appearance:

- ✓ The long upper wick shows the level of price rejection due to high selling pressure or due to absence of buyers price bounced back to the open price.

- ✓ Like hammer it also occurs at the bottom of down trend.
- ✓ It is also considered as a reversal signal of down trend.

How To Trade Inverted Hammer Candle
- ✓ One can take safe entry after confirmation candle once the next candle open above previous closing. Putting low of inverted hammer as a Stop-loss.

Some important points to be note down before entering in an inverted hammer trade.

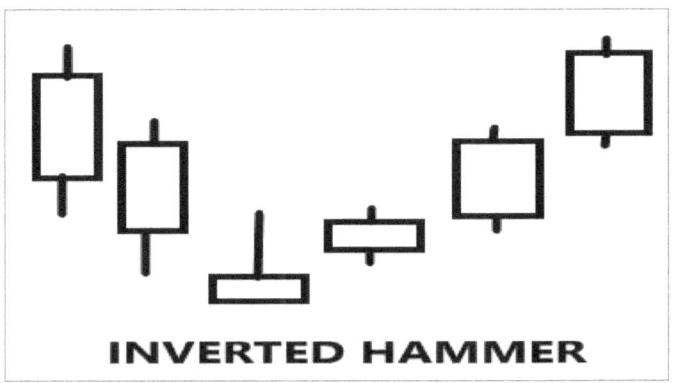

- ✓ Avoid taking entry if risk reward is less than 1:2
- ✓ Longer the upper tail size. Higher will be the bullish reversal.
- ✓ Confirmation candle with high volumes is good sign of reversal.
- ✓ Bullish inverted hammer is better than bearish inverted hammer.

Shooting Star Candle

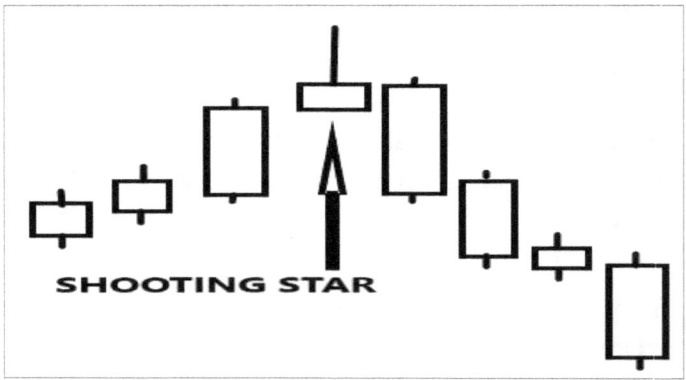

Shooting star is a signal of bearish reversal pattern. It can be seen in uptrend when price get rejected from certain point.

What does shooting star interprets?

A candle tells us few things by its appearance:

- ✓ The open low and close of candle are very near to each other.

- ✓ It has long upper tail just like inverted hammer. That shows price rejection from certain level. Here bulls are not interested now who will play the role definitely bears and when bears enter price fall.

- ✓ One thing that creates difference between inverted hammer and shooting star is that inverted hammer forms in down trend where as shooting star forms in uptrend.

How To Trade Shooting Star

✓ One can take entry in the next candle opening blow or at the closing price of shooting star.

✓ We can put stop-loss above the high of shooting star.

✓ Target should be the immediate support of pattern.

Some important points to be note down before entering in a shooting star trade.

✓ Use other indicators like volume, RSI etc. for more accuracy and confirmation.

✓ If the range between open and close is large resulting in a big stop-loss. We can trail stop- loss after next candle to half of the upper tail of shooting star.

✓ Candle stick must form near resistance and should be bearish (red).

✓ The intensity of reversal depends of the smaller size of shooting star body.

Morning star candle

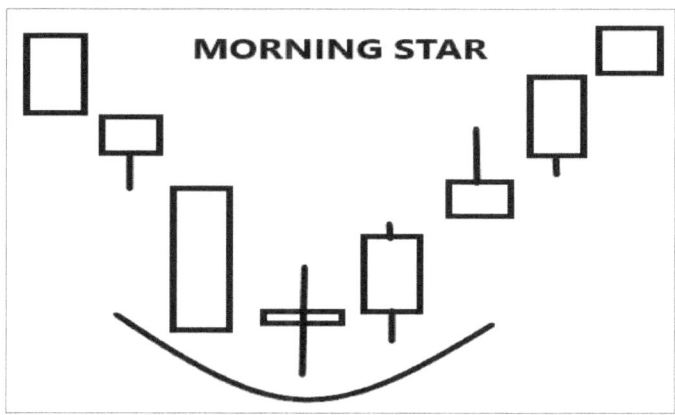

Morning star is the hope of bulls. It is the signal of trend reversal. It forms at the bottom of downtrend. Compose of three candles.

What does morning star interprets?

Candle tells us few things by its appearance:

- ✓ Three candles appearing at the bottom of down trend.
- ✓ It is the signal of trend reversal.
- ✓ First candle should be big red bearish candle of down trend.
- ✓ The middle candle should be small bodied confusing candle either Doji or spinning top. at this point of time both are in back foot. It can be bearish or bullish.
- ✓ The third candle should be bullish with at least half of first candle length.
- ✓ As we discussed all three candle has logic 1st shows bearishness 2nd shows condition of indecision or confusion and the 3rd bullish candle shows the upward move as a trend reversal.

How To Trade Morning Star

- ✓ One can enter above the high of third candle.
- ✓ Stop-loss should be place blow the lower wick of middle candle and target should be the immediate resistance of price action.

Important points should be note down before entering in a morning star trade.

- ✓ Use volume, RSI or any other indicator for more accuracy and confirmation.
- ✓ Remember morning star forms at the bottom of down trend not in uptrend.
- ✓ In case of big stop-loss we can modify it to the low of 3rd candle.
- ✓ The first candle should be red second may be red or green, and the third one must be green with good volume covering half of the length of first candle.

Evening Star Candle

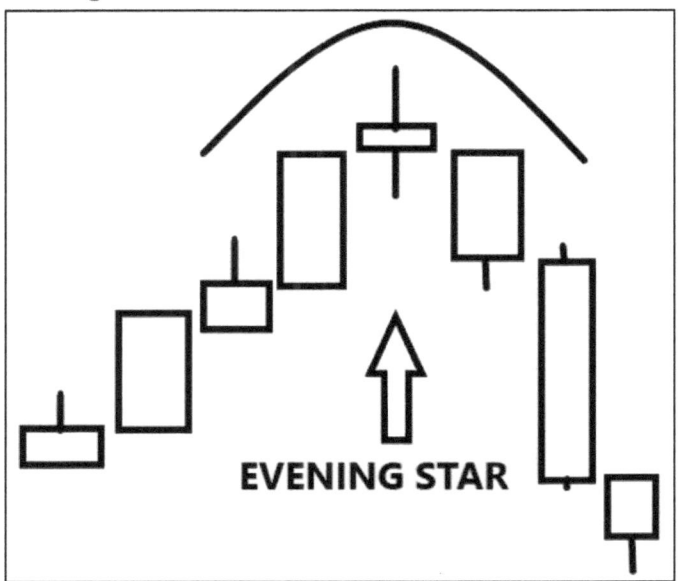

Evening star is just opposite to the morning star. It is the hope of bears. It forms at the top uptrend and is a signal of trend reversal.

What does evening star interprets?

Candle tells us few things by its appearance:

- ✓ It forms with the combination of three candles.
- ✓ 1st candle long bodied bullish candle, 2nd Doji or spinning top, and the 3rd one should be bearish with half of 1st candle length.
- ✓ All three combine shows the trend reversal.

How To Trade Evening Star Candle

- ✓ Entry after confirmation candle at the opening of next candle.
- ✓ We can put stop-loss above the 3rd candle high.
- ✓ Target should be the immediate support of price pattern action.

Some important points should be note down before entering in an evening star trade:

- ✓ Use volume, RSI or any other indicator for more accuracy and confirmation.
- ✓ Remember evening star forms at the top of uptrend and is the signal of trend reversal.
- ✓ The 3rd candle must be bearish with good volume.
- ✓ Avoid trade in condition of less than 1:2 risk rewards.

Hanging Man Candle

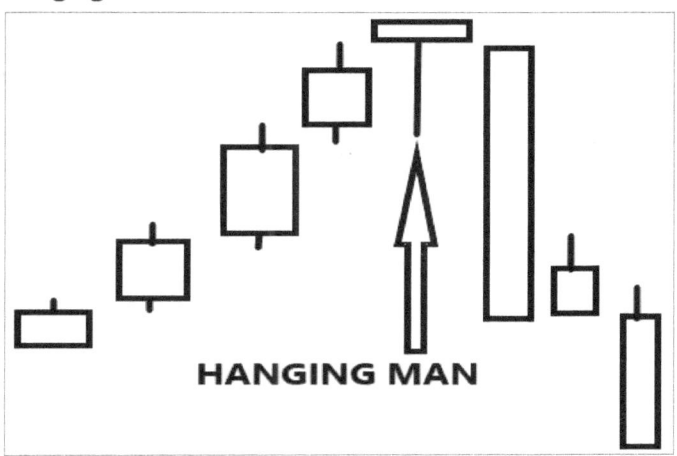

The end of Uptrend is shown by hanging man. it forms near to the resistance level of price action shows that the buyers are exhausted now and not interested and sellers are stronger to lead the race.

What does hanging man interprets?

Candle tells us few things by its appearance:

- ✓ Buyers are not interested more to keep moving price in uptrend.
- ✓ Sellers are strong enough to bring price down now.
- ✓ It forms in continuous uptrend.

How To Trade Hanging Man

✓ Entry after confirmation at the opening of next candle.

✓ Stop-loss should be place at the high of hanging man.

✓ Target should be the immediate support of price action.

Some important should be note down before entering in a hanging man trade:

✓ Use of volume, RSI or another indicator for more accuracy and confirmation.

✓ Hanging man forms at the top of uptrend unlike hammer candle.

✓ The real body must be smaller than the shadow.

✓ The range of candle should be long.

Doji Candle

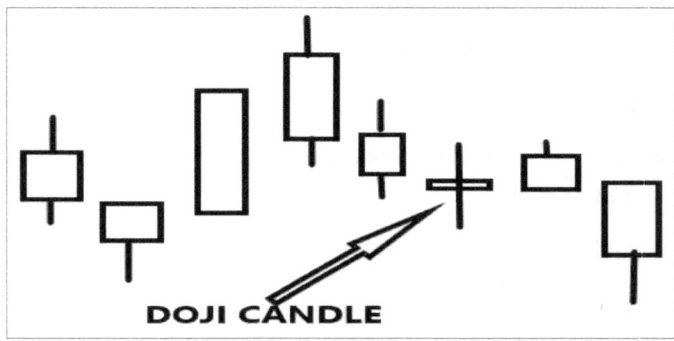

Doji is the result of bulls and bears non resultant fight. Okay let explain it in simple words when bulls attempt to push price up and bears attempts to pull price down and the price closes near to opening price than this directionless movement creates doji candle.

This is the condition of confusion market can go anywhere at this point of time.

There are various types of Doji candles and they are named on the basis of their shape. They are

- ✓ Common Doji.
- ✓ Dragonfly Doji.
- ✓ Gravestone Doji.
- ✓ Long-legged Doji.
- ✓ Four Price Doji.

You can refer image for batter understanding.

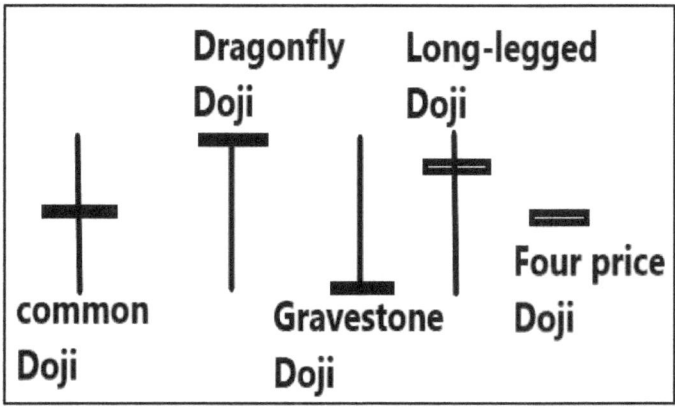

Points To Be Remember Trading Doji Candle.

- ✓ As discussed above Doji candles are sign of confusion in the market. Thus we don't trade Doji alone. When it makes combination with other candle type than it gives signal of trend reversal or trend continuation.

- Morning star.
- Evening Star.

Bullish Engulfing Candle

Engulfing candles are the combination of two candles. One bearish and other bullish.

Bullish Engulfing candle is the combination of two candles. A big bearish candle followed by a bigger bullish candle.

What does Bullish engulfing candle interprets?

Candle tells us few things by appearance:

- ✓ When first candle closes bearish and next bullish candle engulf the first one by closing above the previous candle high. It clearly shows that now market is in the condition of reversal bears lost the game and bulls start dominating.
- ✓ If bullish engulfing pattern forms in uptrend than it is the sign of continuation.
- ✓ If it forms in down trend than it's the sign of trend reversal.

How To Trade Bullish Engulfing Candle

✓ Take entry after confirmation you can use various indicators for confirmation and accuracy.

✓ Stop-loss should be place blow the bullish candle low.

✓ Target should be the immediate resistance in condition of all time high one should use 1:2 concept with trailing stop-loss strategy.

Some important points should be note down before entering in a bullish engulfing candle trade.

✓ Formation of bullish engulf candle in down trend is a signal of trend reversal.

✓ Formation of bullish engulf candle in uptrend is a signal of trend continuation.

✓ Entry after confirmation candle with good volume is considered safer.

Bearish Engulfing Candle

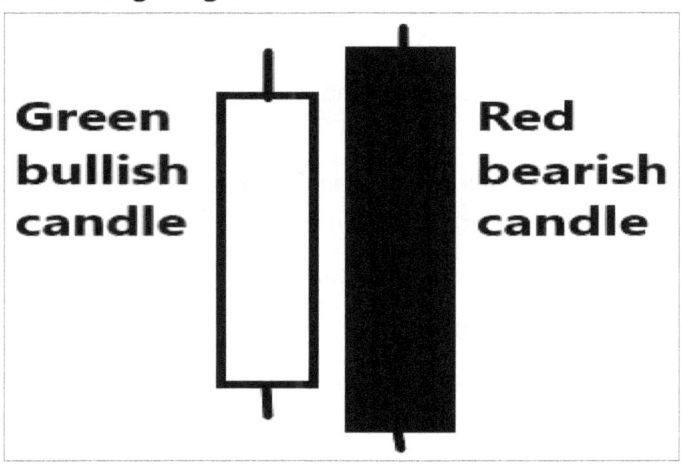

Its looks like bullish engulf only difference is that the 1st candle is bullish which is followed by bearish candle engulfing first one.

What does bearish engulf candle interprets?

Candle tells us few things by appearance:

- ✓ When the second bearish candle closes blow the first bullish candle. Engulfing it completely. it clearly tells us that bears overpowered bulls and now it's a trend reversal of uptrend.
- ✓ If bearish engulfing candle forms in an uptrend
- ✓ than it's a signal of trend reversal
- ✓ If it forms in down trend than it's a signal of trend continuation.

How To Trade Bearish Engulfing Pattern

- ✓ Take entry in the next candle open price after confirmation with good volume.
- ✓ Put stop-loss above the high of red bearish candle.
- ✓ Your target should be the immediate support of price action.

Some important points should be note down before entering in a bearish engulfing trade.

- ✓ Use appropriate indicators for confirmation.
- ✓ One should trail stop-loss.
- ✓ If the formation is in uptrend than it's a signal of trend reversal otherwise trend reversal.

Bullish And Bearish Harami

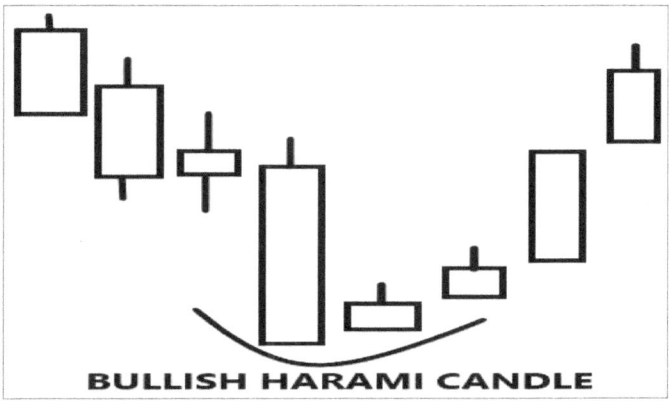

Harami candle is the combination of two candles. The first candle shows the prevailing trend of market where as the second candle is shorter with opposite color. The first candle fully engulfs the second candle.

Bullish Harami Candle

What does bullish Harami candle interprets?

Candle tells us few things by appearance:

- ✓ The 1st big bearish candle tells us about prevailing down trend of market where as the formation of short opposite color candle after long engulfing bearish candle shows defeat of bears and now bulls are ready to lead market after the confirmation of Bullish harami candle.

- ✓ As this upward movement confirms the short covering. Thus price will rise.

How To Trade Bullish Harami Candle

Take entry at the next candle opening price. You can use volume indicator for confirmation.

Put stop-loss blow the low of bullish harami candle.

Your target should be the immediate resistance of price action.

Bearish Harami Candle

It's a bearish harami pattern appears at the top of uptrend. Like bullish harami it also forms with the combination of two candles. Only difference is the first candle is bullish here and second is bearish giving signal of trend reversal.

What does bearish harami candle interprets?

Candle tells us few things by its appearance:

- ✓ The first big bullish candle shows buyers interest in uptrend market.
- ✓ The next bearish candle which is fully engulfed by bullish candle shows the victory of bears and gives a signal of trend reversal.
- ✓ Bearish harami pattern always forms in a uptrend.

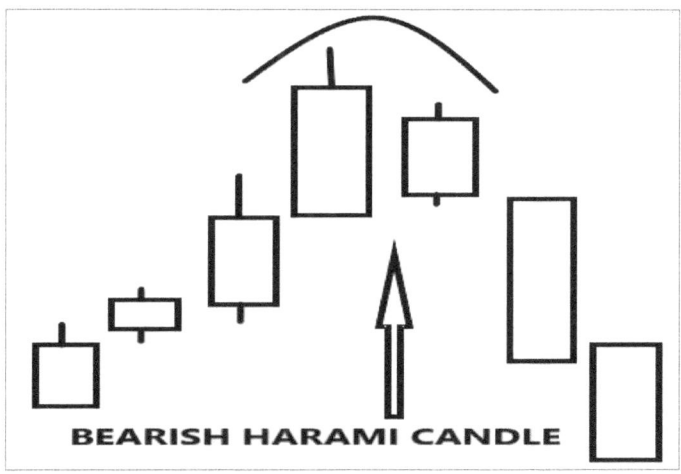

BEARISH HARAMI CANDLE

How To Trade Bearish Harami Candle

✓ Entry after confirmation in the open price of next candle.

✓ Stop-loss should be above the high of second candle

✓ Target should be the immediate support of price action

Some important should be note down before entering in a Bullish harami candle or bearish harami candle trade

✓ The second candle must be engulfed by the first bearish candle (in case of bullish harami) or bullish candle (in case of bearish harami)

✓ Harami candle is the signal of trend reversal.

✓ Only trade after confirmation.

✓ Second candle open gap up (in case of bullish harami), gap down (in case of bearish harami).

Dark Cloud Cover Candle

It is a bearish reversal signal. It is formed by combination of two big candles.

What does dark cloud cover candle interprets?

Candle tells us few things by its appearance:

✓ The first big bullish candle is the sign of prevailing uptrend of market. Whereas the formation of next same size bearish candle tells us that now bears started dominating price and this gives signal of trend reversal.

How To Trade Dark Cover Cloud Candle

✓ We can go selling side in this pattern. Enter blow the close of second candle.

✓ In this candle type stop-loss becomes big and in that condition most of the smart traders avoid trading in the condition of less than 1:2 risk rewards. One should place stop-loss above the high of second bearish candle and trail at cost after 3rd consecutive candle.

✓ Target should be the immediate support of price action.

Some important points to remember before trading dark cloud cover candle.

✓ This formation is a strong signal of trend reversal.

✓ Mostly use to avoid big loss. Least traded.

✓ Take entry only after confirmation also use appropriate indicators for more accuracy.

Piercing Line Candle

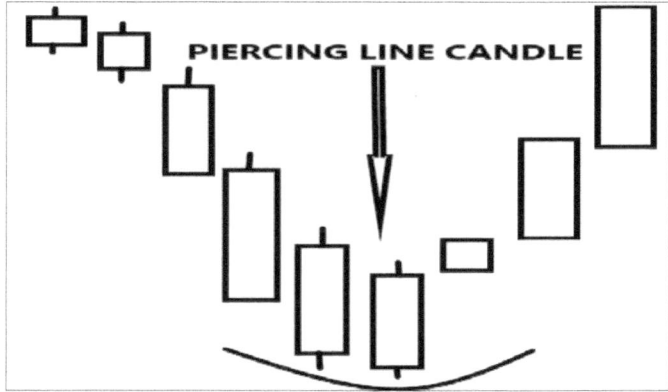

It is a bullish reversal pattern forms at the bottom of down trend, during pull back in uptrend or at near support.

What does piercing line candle interpret?

- ✓ The first bearish candle shows prevailing down trend.
- ✓ The next candle opens gap down and closed as a bullish candle gives signal of trend reversal.
- ✓ This pattern is just opposite to dark cloud cover.

How To Trade Piercing Line Candle

- ✓ Take entry after confirmation at the opening of next candle. There must be a bullish candle with good volume.
- ✓ Stop-loss should be placed blow second candle low.
- ✓ Target should be the immediate resistance of price action.

Some important to remember before entering in a piercing line trade:

- ✓ This candle stick pattern forms in a down trend and is a signal of trend reversal.
- ✓ The first candle should be red bearish candle followed by the gap down opened bullish candle.
- ✓ Use appropriate indicators for more accuracy.

Belt hold candle

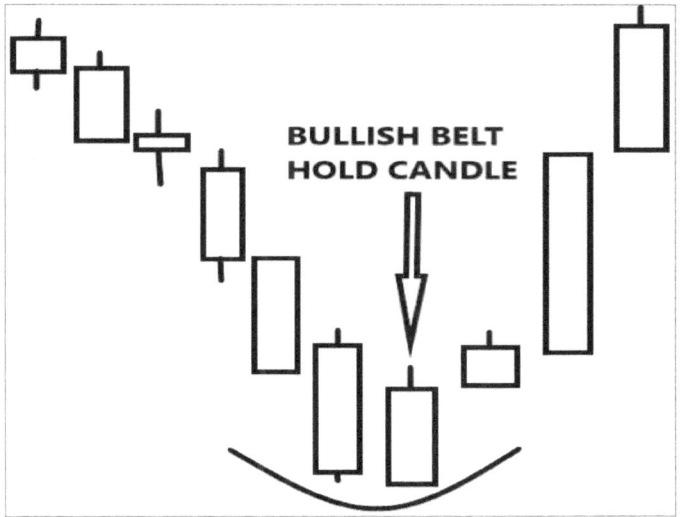

Bullish Belt Hold Candle

Bullish Belt hold is also a trend reversal pattern forms in down trend at the bottom. The combination of two candle looks like piercing line candle only difference is that in belt hold pattern second candle is bullish Morubozu (candle without lower wick).

What does Bullish belt hold candle interpret?

Candle tells us few things by its appearance:

- ✓ The first big bearish candle tells us about prevailing down trend.
- ✓ The next candle should be bullish Morubozu (candle without lower wick) it shows end of down trend. Bulls' overpowering bears and now market is in the condition of trend reversal.

How To Trade Belt Hold Candle

✓ Take entry after confirmation at the opening price of next candle.

✓ Put stop-loss blow the low of second candle.

✓ Targetshould be the immediate resistance formed by price action.

Bearish Belt Hold Candle

Unlike bullish belt hold pattern, bearish belt hold candle pattern forms in uptrend and gives signal of trend reversal.

What does bearish belt hold interpret?

Candle tells us few things by its appearance:

✓ The first candle big bullish shows prevailing market trend and the formation of next gap up bearish Morubozu candle gives reversal signal of market trend.

How To Trade Bearish Belt Hold Candle

✓ Take entry after confirmation at the opening price of next bearish candle.

✓ Keep stop-loss high of second candle.

✓ Target should be the immediate support of price action.

Some important points to remember before trading bullish belt hold or bearish belt hold.

✓ Use appropriate indicator for more accuracy and confirmation.

✓ Bullish belt formation can be seen in down trend where as the formation of bearish belt hold can be seen in uptrend.

✓ The second candle in both the condition must be Morubozu. (bullish morubozu in bullish belt hold and bearish Morubozu in bearish belt hold)

Three white soldiers

Three white soldiers candle forms in a down trend or in continuation of uptrend. They give signal of trend reversal in condition of down trend and trend continuation in condition of uptrend. It is a combination of three big green bullish consecutive candles.

What does three white soldiers interprets?

Candle tells us few things by its appearance:

- ✓ The three long consecutive bullish candles show dominance of bulls in market.
- ✓ The consecutive candles open above or within the opening price of previous candle.
- ✓ Each candle closes at or near to its high shows the strength of bullishness.
- ✓ The occurrence of this pattern at the bottom gives clear cut signal of trend reversal.
- ✓ If this pattern appears at the top of uptrend than it gives signal of trend continuation.

How To Trade Three Green Soldiers Candle

- ✓ After the formation of three candles we can take entry in the next opening price.
- ✓ The stop-loss should be blow the low of first candle.
- ✓ Target should be the immediate resistance of price action.

Some important points to remember before trading three white soldiers candle.

✓ We should use volume indicator for confirmation.

✓ If stop-loss becomes big we should use trailing stop-loss technique.

✓ This is a trend reversal pattern forms blow down trend.

✓ The three candles should not have bigger wicks. There wicks must be negligible or no wick.

✓ We should avoid this pattern in condition of over valuation of price. Or in condition of less risk reward.

Three Black Crows

Three black crows candle is just opposite of three white soldiers. This candle combination forms at the top of uptrend and is a signal of trend reversal.

What does three crows candle interprets?

Candle tells us few things by its appearance:

- ✓ The formation of three same sized bearish candles in uptrend tells us that now bears overpowering bulls. It can end uptrend and trend reversal will happen.
- ✓ The formation of these three bearish candles takes place in a consecutive manner. The three candles opens within the body of preceding candle and close lower the preceding candle.
- ✓ These candles closes blow the previous candle having very small or no lower shadow.

How To Trade Three Black Crows Candle Pattern

- ✓ Entry at the opening of next candle. You can use volume indicator for confirmation.
- ✓ Stop-loss should be above the high of first candle.
- ✓ Target should be the immediate support of price action.

Some important points to remember before trading three black crows candle.

- ✓ This is a trend reversal pattern.
- ✓ In condition of big stop-loss or low volume avoid trade.
- ✓ Use volume, RSI or any other indicator for more confirmation and accuracy.

How To Draw Trend Line

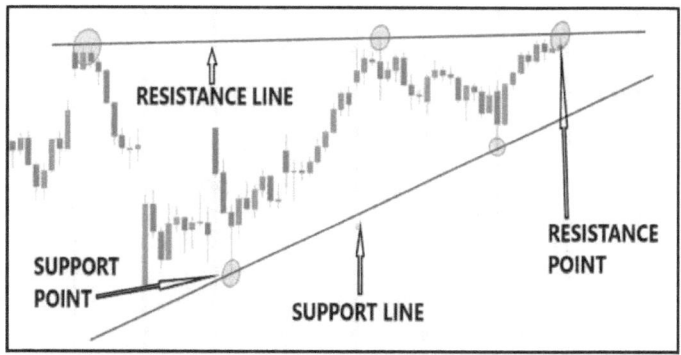

Trend lines are vertical or sloping lines joining support or resistance points in a chart.

How To Draw Trade Line

For intraday trading most preferred time frames are 5 min and 15 min-

- Step 1- find out support and resistance points.
- Step 2- multiple time frame analysis of identified support and resistance points.

- Step 3- join all support points through a line resultant will be a support line. Join all resistance points resultant will be a resistance line.

Demand And Supply Zone

Demand zone – the range of price form where heavy buying happens (buying range).

Supply zone- the range of price from where heavy selling happens (selling range).

How To Draw Demand And Supply Zone

- Finding support and resistance range by multiple time frame analysis.
- Using rectangle joining all support and resistance points.
- Resistance points may be high, close or open
- Support points may be low, close or open.

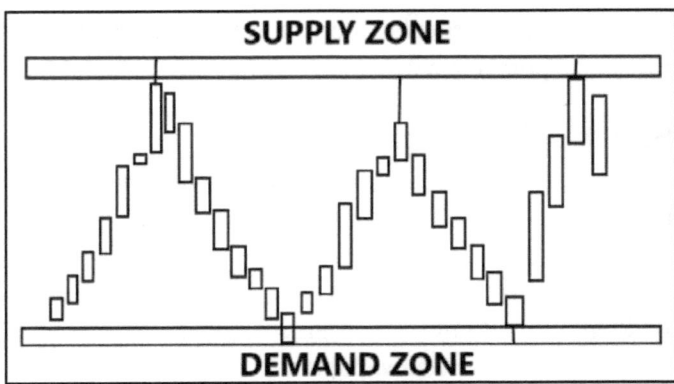

Understanding Price Patterns

Price patterns are various patterns formed by the movement of price. The configuration of these price movement forms a recognizable pattern we identify or draw price pattern with the help of trend lines, curves etc.

What does price pattern interprets?

- ✓ Change in price can be predicted with the help of price patterns.
- ✓ They give us signal of trend reversal and trend continuation.
- ✓ Price pattern forms in the configuration of price movement.
- ✓ Price pattern gives us price direction price rise or price fall. Depending on the side of brake out.

Various Types Of Price Patterns

We can categories price patterns into three types on the basis of their interpretation.

1. Bullish pattern
2. Bearish pattern
3. Reversal pattern

Bullish Patterns

These patterns mostly form in uptrend gives signal of price rise Or trend continuation

- Flag
- Pennant
- Cup&handle
- Ascending Triangle
- Symmetrical Triangle
- Measured Move Up
- Ascending Scallop
- 3 Raising Valley

Bearish Pattern
- Flag
- Pennant
- Inverted Cup&handle
- Descending Triangle
- Symmetrical Triangle
- Measured Move Down
- Descending Scallop
- 3 Descending Peaks

Reversal Pattern
- Double bottoms
- Diamond bottom
- Tops rectangle
- Head&Shoulders Top

Flag pattern
- Two parallel lines they may be slope up, slope down or horizontal (side base).
- This pattern gives signal of trend continuation after consolidation.
- When this pattern appears in uptrend it's called
- bullish flag.
- When this pattern forms in down trend called bearish flag.

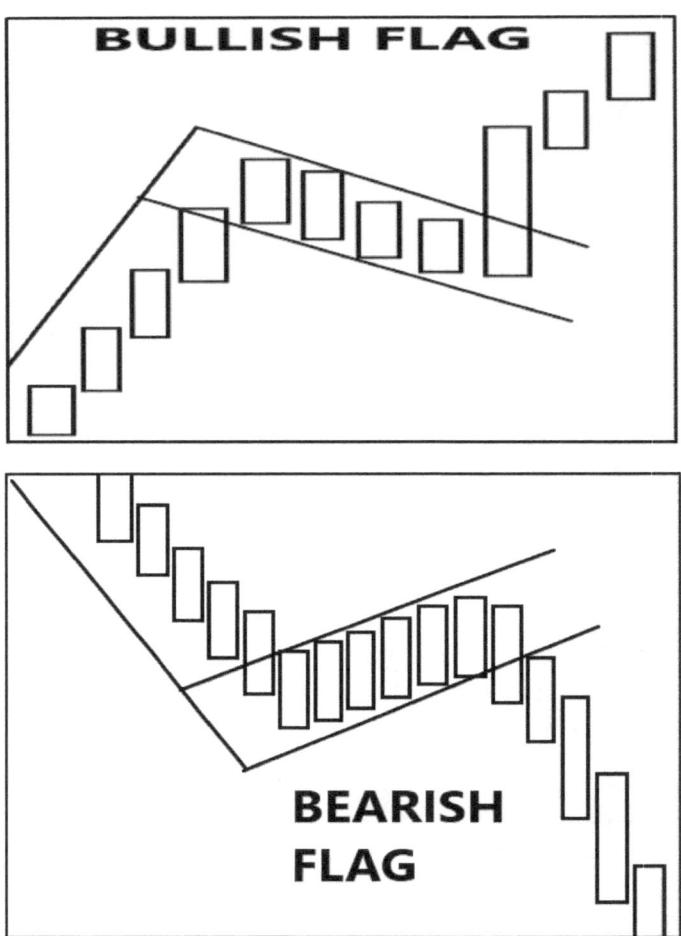

Pennant Pattern

- When price goes in a large upward movement and after a brief consolidation continue movement in the same direction. This consolidation resembles a symmetrical triangle shape called pennant. This is a continuation pattern.

- When this pattern forms in uptrend it is considered as bullish pennant.
- When this pattern forms in downtrend considered as bearish pennant.

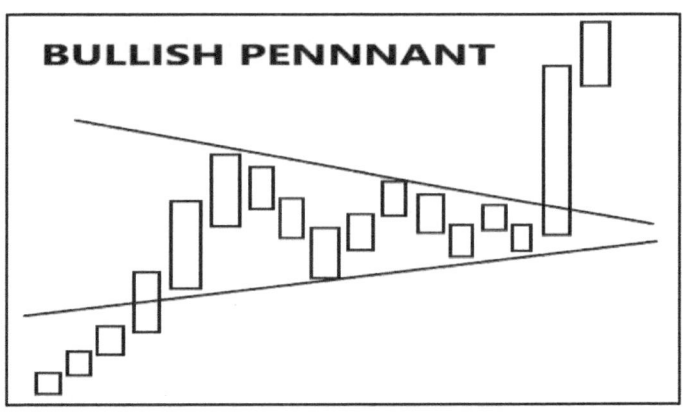

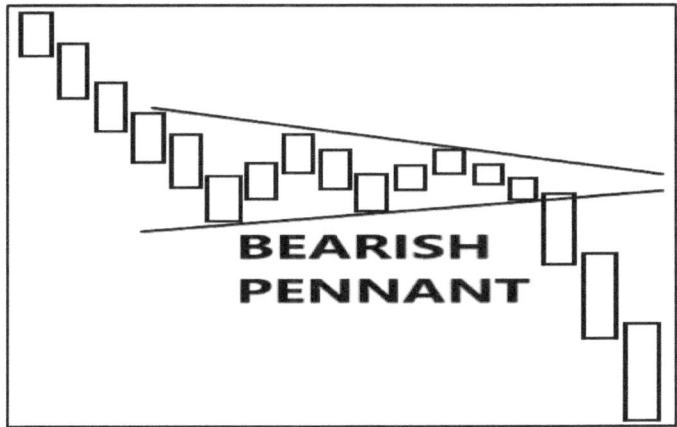

Cup & Handle Pattern

- The movement of price resembles shape of a cup with handle.

- In uptrend when price fall and came back to the previous level after little consolidation continue moving in same trend. Cup & handle pattern can be seen.

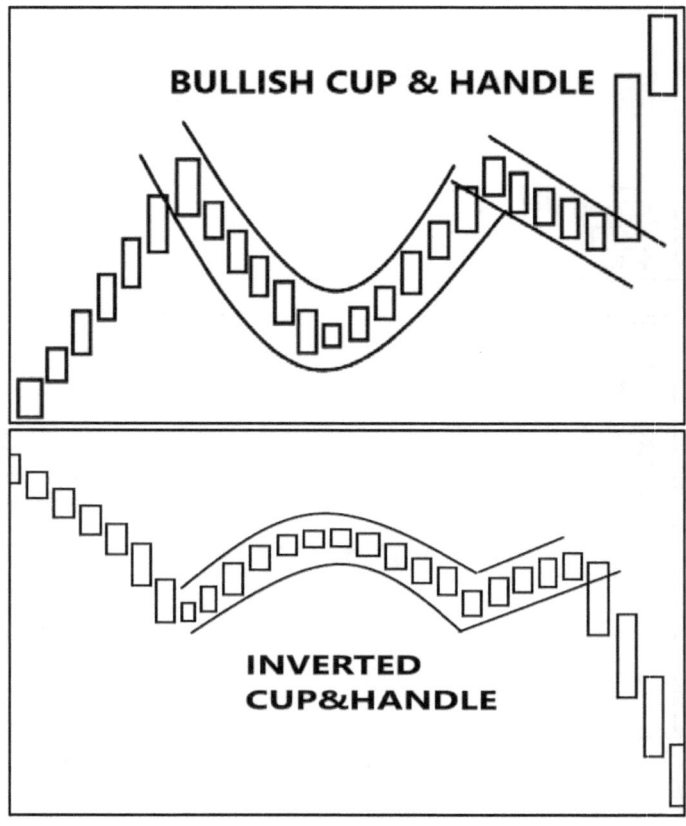

Ascending Triangle Pattern

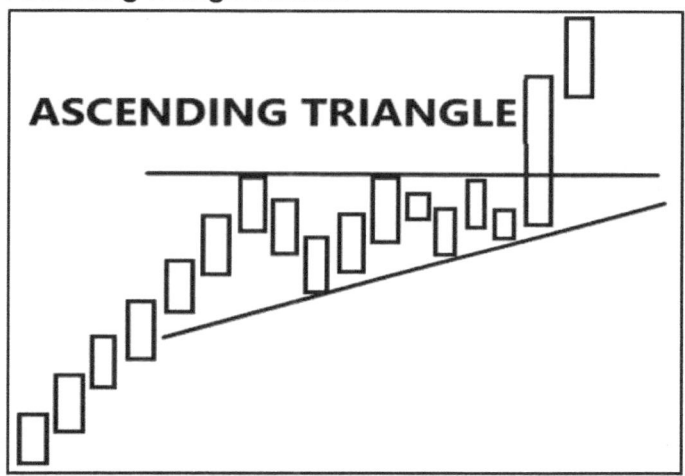

- This pattern appears in uptrend when after little consolidation price continue movement in upward direction.
- The consolidation resembles the shape of ascending triangle thus named ascending triangle pattern.

Symmetrical Triangle Pattern

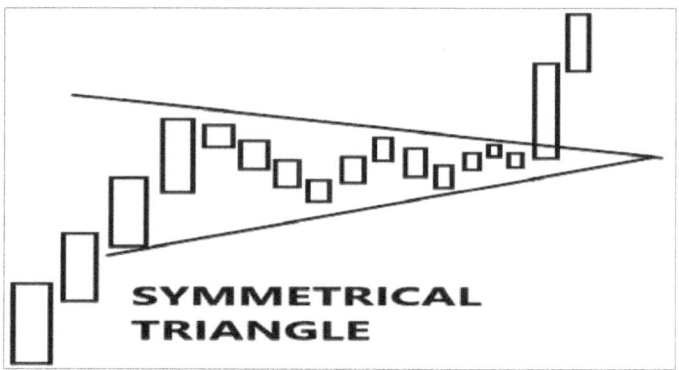

- When the resistance and support lines converge and meet at a point middle of consolidation such shape resembles the shape of symmetrical triangle.
- This pattern gives signal of trend continuation.
- In symmetrical triangle we get brake outs both side. Thus it may be continuation or reversal both.

Measured Move Up Pattern

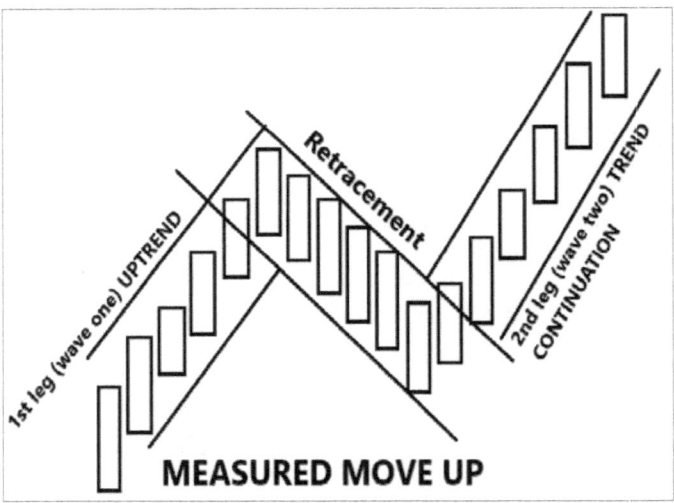

- This pattern has three parts first part called 1st leg (wave one) the upward movement of price (uptrend) followed by retracement than 2nd leg (wave two) which shows the continuation of uptrend.

- One common difference between measured move up and Flag pattern is in flag pattern trend continuation happen after consolidation unlike in measured move up in which retracement (pull back) happens.

Measured Move Down

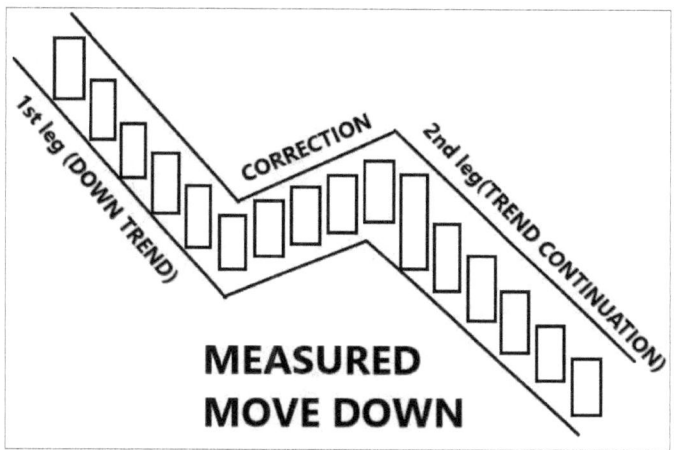

- This pattern can be divided into three parts 1st leg which shows prevailing down trend in the market than small correction in price followed by 2nd leg continuation of down trend.

Ascending Scallop Pattern

- This pattern appears in uptrend or in side base market and gives signal of price rise.
- At the beginning the price drops little after little consolidation starts moving in uptrend. It forms J shape price pattern.

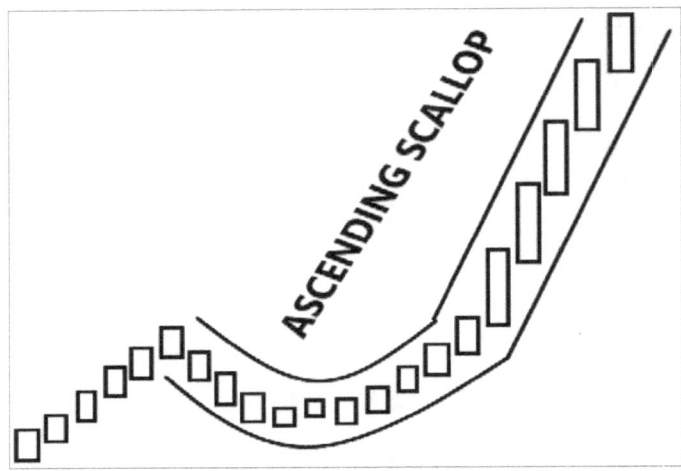

Descending Scallop Pattern

- This pattern appears in down or in side base market and gives signal of price fall.
- At the beginning price shows little correction and consolidation after that starts moving in down trend. It forms mirror image of J.

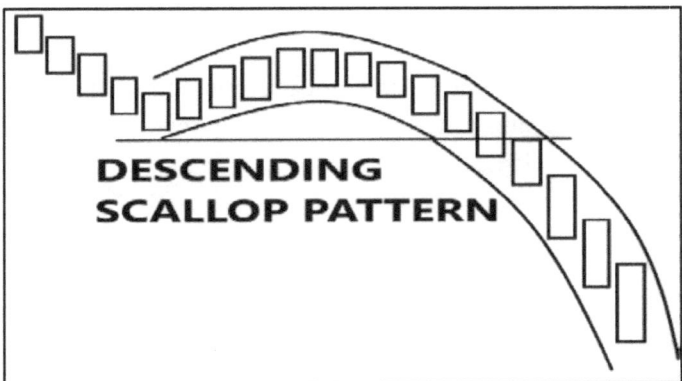

Three Raising Valley Pattern

- This pattern can be seen in both trends. It has three valleys. The second valley low is higher than the first valley and the third valley low higher than second valley.

- It has two peaks the second peak high is higher than the first Peak.

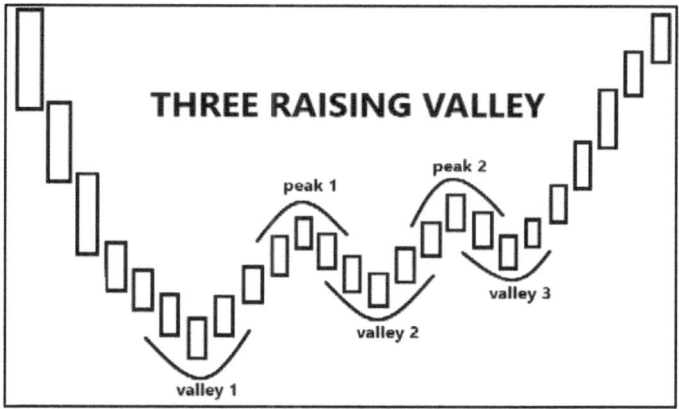

Three Falling Peaks

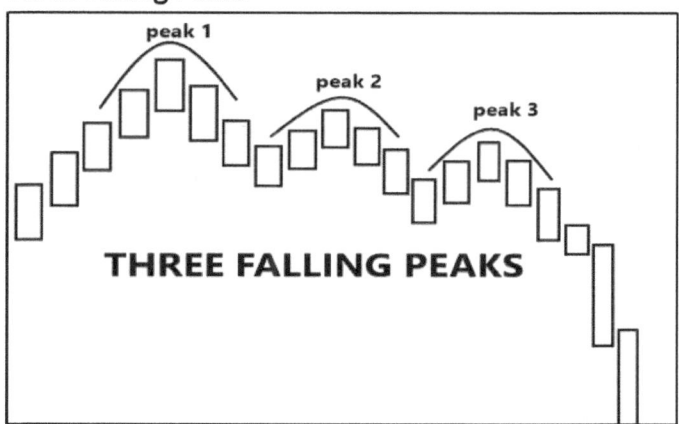

- It has three peaks the high of second peak is lower than first peak and high of third peak is lower than second peak. It also has two valleys making lower lows.
- The shapes of all peaks are similar and second valley has lower low than first valley.
- It is the signal of price fall in case of downtrend continuation may happen.

Double Bottom Pattern

- It is a bullish reversal pattern forms after down trend. It gives signal of price rise
- In down trend after rejection price shows some correction making first bottom after that price fall again making new swing low (Second bottom) equal to first low.
- When price breaks resistances in second bounce it gives signal of trend reversal (price rise).

Diamond Bottom Pattern

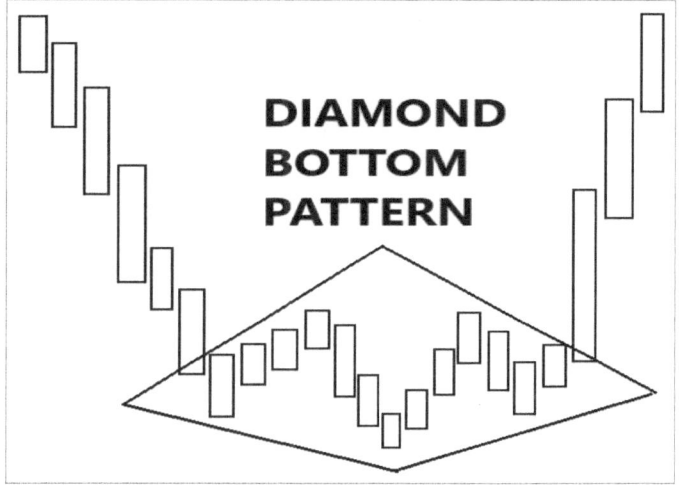

- It is a bullish reversal pattern. Forms after down trend.
- Its shape resembles combination of two symmetrical triangles side by side.
- It price action expands from left side than start contracting at narrow range until brake out. Forming shape like diamond.

Rectangle Pattern

- This pattern gives signal of trend reversal.
- It forms after uptrend (top rectangle) or downtrend (Bottom rectangle).
- In this pattern price fluctuate between support and resistance line. After brake out price show signal of trend reversal.
- It has parallel tops and bottoms.

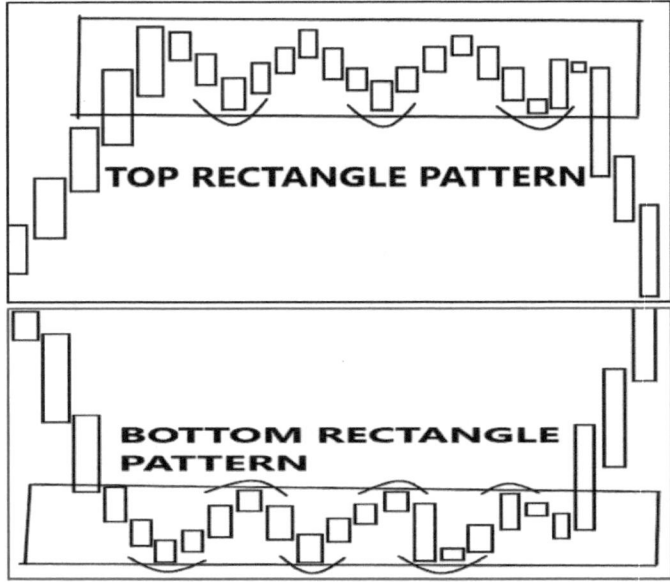

Head & Shoulders Pattern

- This is a trend reversal pattern.

- It has resembles shape of head and shoulders having three mountain shape price structures. Two of similar sizes lift and right the middle mountain is quite bigger than two.

- Top head & shoulders is a signal of price fall where as bottom head & shoulders signals price rise.

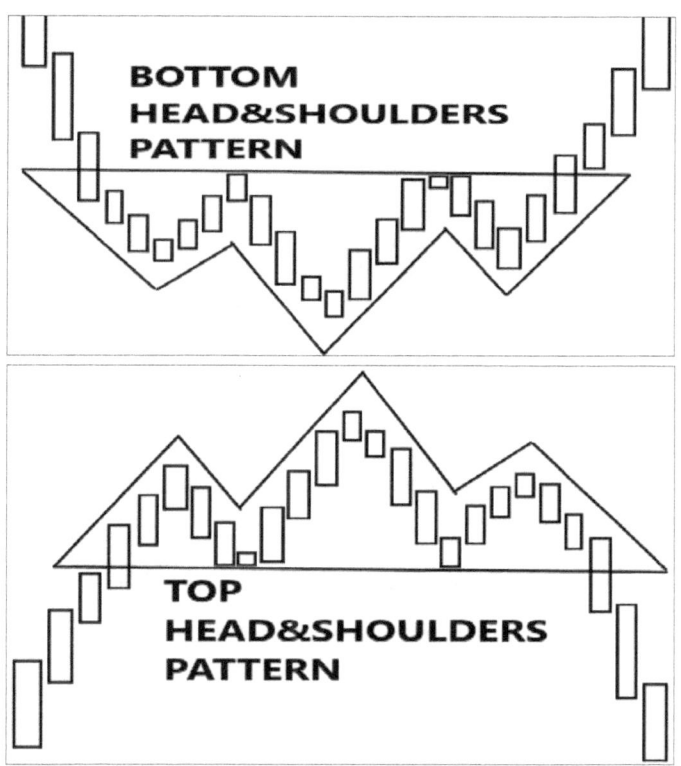

How To Identify Right Brake Out

- There are few points which will help you to find right brake out.
- Your resistance and support points must be respected by price action.
- Trend line must be broke with good volume.
- You can use volume indicator for confirmation.
- The candle which brake resistance or support line must not have bigger wick.
- Next candle open must be higher in case of resistance and lower in case of support.
- You can also use RSI indicator for more confirmation.
- Remember one thing our previous resistance becomes new support and previous supports become new resistance. Thus this law must be respected by price action.

Fear & Greed

Fear and greed are both in the nature of man, we cannot remove them, and if someone says that I can remove them, then it will be a foolish thing because it is impossible to remove them, we come somewhere at one point and fall prey to them. That's why we should use our fear and greed in the right place at the right time but in the right limit. Now it comes to why fear and greed are necessary and what is their importance.

For a monk, these two emotions may be insignificant, but both these emotions have a different importance in the life of a trader and businessman.

So what is the significance of these two emotions?

Fear saves us, fear stops us, advises us to act according to our ability, at the same way greed drives us forward, greed pushes us to move forward.

Desire to do something and get something comes from lack of things and influence.

Controlling emotions is not an easy task it requires tireless efforts and a curiosity to learn and move forward continuously.

Meditation is the only way through which you can control both these emotions and learn to use them properly.

Learn And Earn With Market's Move

We get learning from mistakes. Now these mistakes may be done by our self or by others. We have to learn from every mistake and move on. It is not an easy task. Many times the mistakes made in the market can cost us a lot. We have to take special care that any mistake made by us should not throw us out of the market.

One thing I have understood while being in the market for so long is that trading or becoming a professional trader depends on an individual.

People can give you information; they may teach you something, share strategy, can give tips or advice. But all these things are not sufficient for becoming a trader. Becoming a trader is a step-by-step process that takes time. Trading is a multi-dimensional process it has various dimensions like trading psychology, analysis, money management, risk management etc. thus it becomes necessary for a trader to develop himself in various dimensions involve in trading. It is very practical thing which you will learn when you will live with market. So survival should be the first priority you can survive by protecting our profits, reducing our losses or any other method which suits you. What I did I made charts my friends and market my Guru. And learning and earning with markets move.

Who Is The Boss?

Market itself is the BOSS neither institutions nor retail traders. It is very necessary to understand markets mood when we plan our day we have to act according to market if market is bullish we become bull if market is bearish we become bear. A trader should not act opposite to the market.

Things to remember:

1. Follow the trend if market is in uptrend it will go up. If market is in down trend it will go down.
2. Do not trade in a side base market. Trading in a side base market is like gambling in a casino.
3. Always try to invest trading earned amount in safer instruments. Do not put that amount in same risk which you took to earn that profit
4. Never ever try to predict market because it is unpredictable.
5. Some time a trader comes in ego if market goes opposite to his analysis he keeps fighting with the market. We should avoid ego trading either close our position at minimum loss or move with market's mood.
6. Always work with numbers not with the rates. Because when we work on money our emotions start involving with it.

Trading Journal 100 Day's Trading Challenge To Improve Our Trading

Date			Day			
Segment	Quantity	Buying Price	Selling Price	Target Or Stoploss	Risk/ Reward	Profit/Loss

Total Profit/Loss	
Charges	
Brokerage	
STT	
Other Charges	
Total Charges	
Grand Total (Profit - Total Charges/Loss + Total Charges)	

Remark

Market Movement		Mistakes	
Balance B/D		**Balance C/D**	

Observations

Trading खाता

Date				Day			
Segment	Quantity	Buying Price	Selling Price	Target Or Stoploss	Risk/ Reward	Profit/Loss

Total Profit/Loss	
Charges	
Brokerage	
STT	
Other Charges	
Total Charges	
Grand Total (Profit - Total Charges/Loss + Total Charges)	

Remark

Market Movement		Mistakes	
Balance B/D		Balance C/D	

Observations

Date			Day			
Segment	Quantity	Buying Price	Selling Price	Target Or Stoploss	Risk/ Reward	Profit/Loss

Total Profit/Loss	
Charges	
Brokerage	
STT	
Other Charges	
Total Charges	
Grand Total (Profit - Total Charges/Loss + Total Charges)	

Remark

Market Movement		Mistakes	
Balance B/D		**Balance C/D**	

Observations

Trading खाता

Date				Day			
Segment	Quantity	Buying Price	Selling Price	Target Or Stoploss		Risk/ Reward	Profit/Loss

Total Profit/Loss	
Charges	
Brokerage	
STT	
Other Charges	
Total Charges	
Grand Total (Profit - Total Charges/Loss + Total Charges)	

Remark

Market Movement		Mistakes	
Balance B/D		Balance C/D	

Observations

Date			Day			
Segment	Quantity	Buying Price	Selling Price	Target Or Stoploss	Risk/ Reward	Profit/Loss

Total Profit/Loss	
Charges	
Brokerage	
STT	
Other Charges	
Total Charges	
Grand Total (Profit - Total Charges/Loss + Total Charges)	

Remark

Market Movement		Mistakes	
Balance B/D		Balance C/D	

Observations

Trading खाता

Date				Day			
Segment	Quantity	Buying Price	Selling Price	Target Or Stoploss		Risk/ Reward	Profit/Loss
Total Profit/Loss							
Charges							
Brokerage							
STT							
Other Charges							
Total Charges							
Grand Total (Profit - Total Charges/Loss + Total Charges)							

Remark

Market Movement		Mistakes	
Balance B/D		**Balance C/D**	

Observations

Date			Day			
Segment	Quantity	Buying Price	Selling Price	Target Or Stoploss	Risk/ Reward	Profit/Loss
Total Profit/Loss						
Charges						
Brokerage						
STT						
Other Charges						
Total Charges						
Grand Total (Profit - Total Charges/Loss + Total Charges)						

Remark

Market Movement		Mistakes	
Balance B/D		Balance C/D	

Observations

Trading खाता

Date				Day			
Segment	Quantity	Buying Price	Selling Price	Target Or Stoploss	Risk/ Reward	Profit/Loss	

Total Profit/Loss	
Charges	
Brokerage	
STT	
Other Charges	
Total Charges	
Grand Total (Profit - Total Charges/Loss + Total Charges)	

Remark

Market Movement		Mistakes	
Balance B/D		**Balance C/D**	

Observations

Date			Day			
Segment	Quantity	Buying Price	Selling Price	Target Or Stoploss	Risk/ Reward	Profit/Loss

Total Profit/Loss	
Charges	
Brokerage	
STT	
Other Charges	
Total Charges	
Grand Total (Profit - Total Charges/Loss + Total Charges)	

Remark

Market Movement		Mistakes	
Balance B/D		Balance C/D	

Observations

Trading खाता

Date			Day			
Segment	Quantity	Buying Price	Selling Price	Target Or Stoploss	Risk/ Reward	Profit/Loss
Total Profit/Loss						
Charges						
Brokerage						
STT						
Other Charges						
Total Charges						
Grand Total (Profit - Total Charges/Loss + Total Charges)						

Remark

Market Movement		Mistakes	
Balance B/D		Balance C/D	

Observations

Date			Day			
Segment	Quantity	Buying Price	Selling Price	Target Or Stoploss	Risk/ Reward	Profit/Loss

Total Profit/Loss	
Charges	
Brokerage	
STT	
Other Charges	
Total Charges	
Grand Total (Profit - Total Charges/Loss + Total Charges)	

Remark

Market Movement		Mistakes	
Balance B/D		Balance C/D	

Observations

Trading खाता

Date			Day			
Segment	Quantity	Buying Price	Selling Price	Target Or Stoploss	Risk/ Reward	Profit/Loss

Total Profit/Loss	
Charges	
Brokerage	
STT	
Other Charges	
Total Charges	
Grand Total (Profit - Total Charges/Loss + Total Charges)	

Remark

Market Movement		Mistakes	
Balance B/D		Balance C/D	

Observations

Date			Day			
Segment	Quantity	Buying Price	Selling Price	Target Or Stoploss	Risk/ Reward	Profit/Loss

Total Profit/Loss	
Charges	
Brokerage	
STT	
Other Charges	
Total Charges	
Grand Total (Profit - Total Charges/Loss + Total Charges)	

Remark

Market Movement		Mistakes	
Balance B/D		Balance C/D	

Observations

Trading खाता

Date				Day			
Segment	Quantity	Buying Price	Selling Price	Target Or Stoploss	Risk/ Reward	Profit/Loss

Total Profit/Loss	
Charges	
Brokerage	
STT	
Other Charges	
Total Charges	
Grand Total (Profit - Total Charges/Loss + Total Charges)	

Remark

Market Movement		Mistakes	
Balance B/D		**Balance C/D**	

Observations

Date				Day			
Segment	Quantity	Buying Price	Selling Price	Target Or Stoploss		Risk/ Reward	Profit/Loss
Total Profit/Loss							
Charges							
Brokerage							
STT							
Other Charges							
Total Charges							
Grand Total (Profit - Total Charges/Loss + Total Charges)							

Remark

Market Movement		Mistakes	
Balance B/D		Balance C/D	

Observations

Trading खाता

Date			Day			
Segment	Quantity	Buying Price	Selling Price	Target Or Stoploss	Risk/ Reward	Profit/Loss

Total Profit/Loss	
Charges	
Brokerage	
STT	
Other Charges	
Total Charges	
Grand Total (Profit - Total Charges/Loss + Total Charges)	

Remark

Market Movement		Mistakes	
Balance B/D		Balance C/D	

Observations

Date			Day			
Segment	Quantity	Buying Price	Selling Price	Target Or Stoploss	Risk/ Reward	Profit/Loss

Total Profit/Loss	
Charges	
Brokerage	
STT	
Other Charges	
Total Charges	
Grand Total (Profit - Total Charges/Loss + Total Charges)	

Remark

Market Movement		Mistakes	
Balance B/D		Balance C/D	

Observations

Trading खाता

Date			Day			
Segment	Quantity	Buying Price	Selling Price	Target Or Stoploss	Risk/ Reward	Profit/Loss

Total Profit/Loss	
Charges	
Brokerage	
STT	
Other Charges	
Total Charges	
Grand Total (Profit - Total Charges/Loss + Total Charges)	

Remark

Market Movement		Mistakes	
Balance B/D		Balance C/D	

Observations

Date			Day			
Segment	Quantity	Buying Price	Selling Price	Target Or Stoploss	Risk/ Reward	Profit/Loss

Total Profit/Loss	
Charges	
Brokerage	
STT	
Other Charges	
Total Charges	
Grand Total (Profit - Total Charges/Loss + Total Charges)	

Remark

Market Movement		Mistakes	
Balance B/D		Balance C/D	

Observations

Trading खाता

Date				Day			
Segment	Quantity	Buying Price	Selling Price	Target Or Stoploss	Risk/ Reward	Profit/Loss

Total Profit/Loss	
Charges	
Brokerage	
STT	
Other Charges	
Total Charges	
Grand Total (Profit - Total Charges/Loss + Total Charges)	

Remark

Market Movement		Mistakes	
Balance B/D		Balance C/D	

Observations

Date			Day			
Segment	Quantity	Buying Price	Selling Price	Target Or Stoploss	Risk/ Reward	Profit/Loss

Total Profit/Loss	
Charges	
Brokerage	
STT	
Other Charges	
Total Charges	
Grand Total (Profit - Total Charges/Loss + Total Charges)	

Remark

Market Movement		Mistakes	
Balance B/D		Balance C/D	

Observations

Trading खाता

Date			Day			
Segment	Quantity	Buying Price	Selling Price	Target Or Stoploss	Risk/ Reward	Profit/Loss

Total Profit/Loss	
Charges	
Brokerage	
STT	
Other Charges	
Total Charges	
Grand Total (Profit - Total Charges/Loss + Total Charges)	

Remark

Market Movement		Mistakes	
Balance B/D		Balance C/D	

Observations

Date			Day			
Segment	Quantity	Buying Price	Selling Price	Target Or Stoploss	Risk/ Reward	Profit/Loss

Total Profit/Loss	
Charges	
Brokerage	
STT	
Other Charges	
Total Charges	
Grand Total (Profit - Total Charges/Loss + Total Charges)	

Remark

Market Movement		Mistakes	
Balance B/D		Balance C/D	

Observations

Trading खाता

Date			Day			
Segment	Quantity	Buying Price	Selling Price	Target Or Stoploss	Risk/ Reward	Profit/Loss
Total Profit/Loss						
Charges						
Brokerage						
STT						
Other Charges						
Total Charges						
Grand Total (Profit - Total Charges/Loss + Total Charges)						

Remark

Market Movement		Mistakes	
Balance B/D		**Balance C/D**	

Observations

Date			Day			
Segment	Quantity	Buying Price	Selling Price	Target Or Stoploss	Risk/ Reward	Profit/Loss

Total Profit/Loss	
Charges	
Brokerage	
STT	
Other Charges	
Total Charges	
Grand Total (Profit - Total Charges/Loss + Total Charges)	

Remark

Market Movement		Mistakes	
Balance B/D		Balance C/D	

Observations

Trading खाता

Date			Day			
Segment	Quantity	Buying Price	Selling Price	Target Or Stoploss	Risk/ Reward	Profit/Loss

Total Profit/Loss	
Charges	
Brokerage	
STT	
Other Charges	
Total Charges	
Grand Total (Profit - Total Charges/Loss + Total Charges)	

Remark

Market Movement		Mistakes	
Balance B/D		Balance C/D	

Observations

Date			Day			
Segment	Quantity	Buying Price	Selling Price	Target Or Stoploss	Risk/ Reward	Profit/Loss

Total Profit/Loss	
Charges	
Brokerage	
STT	
Other Charges	
Total Charges	
Grand Total (Profit - Total Charges/Loss + Total Charges)	

Remark

Market Movement		Mistakes	
Balance B/D		Balance C/D	

Observations

Trading खाता

Date			Day			
Segment	Quantity	Buying Price	Selling Price	Target Or Stoploss	Risk/ Reward	Profit/Loss
Total Profit/Loss						
Charges						
Brokerage						
STT						
Other Charges						
Total Charges						
Grand Total (Profit - Total Charges/Loss + Total Charges)						

Remark

Market Movement		Mistakes	
Balance B/D		Balance C/D	

Observations

Date			Day			
Segment	Quantity	Buying Price	Selling Price	Target Or Stoploss	Risk/ Reward	Profit/Loss

Total Profit/Loss	
Charges	
Brokerage	
STT	
Other Charges	
Total Charges	
Grand Total (Profit - Total Charges/Loss + Total Charges)	

Remark

Market Movement		Mistakes	
Balance B/D		Balance C/D	

Observations

Trading खाता

Date			Day			
Segment	Quantity	Buying Price	Selling Price	Target Or Stoploss	Risk/ Reward	Profit/Loss
Total Profit/Loss						
Charges						
Brokerage						
STT						
Other Charges						
Total Charges						
Grand Total (Profit - Total Charges/Loss + Total Charges)						

Remark

Market Movement		Mistakes	
Balance B/D		**Balance C/D**	

Observations

Date			Day			
Segment	Quantity	Buying Price	Selling Price	Target Or Stoploss	Risk/ Reward	Profit/Loss

Total Profit/Loss	
Charges	
Brokerage	
STT	
Other Charges	
Total Charges	
Grand Total (Profit - Total Charges/Loss + Total Charges)	

Remark

Market Movement		Mistakes	
Balance B/D		Balance C/D	

Observations

Trading खाता

Date			Day			
Segment	Quantity	Buying Price	Selling Price	Target Or Stoploss	Risk/ Reward	Profit/Loss

Total Profit/Loss	
Charges	
Brokerage	
STT	
Other Charges	
Total Charges	
Grand Total (Profit - Total Charges/Loss + Total Charges)	

Remark

Market Movement		Mistakes	
Balance B/D		Balance C/D	

Observations

Date			Day			
Segment	Quantity	Buying Price	Selling Price	Target Or Stoploss	Risk/ Reward	Profit/Loss

Total Profit/Loss	
Charges	
Brokerage	
STT	
Other Charges	
Total Charges	
Grand Total (Profit - Total Charges/Loss + Total Charges)	

Remark

Market Movement		Mistakes	
Balance B/D		Balance C/D	

Observations

Trading खाता

Date			Day			
Segment	Quantity	Buying Price	Selling Price	Target Or Stoploss	Risk/ Reward	Profit/Loss

Total Profit/Loss	
Charges	
Brokerage	
STT	
Other Charges	
Total Charges	
Grand Total (Profit - Total Charges/Loss + Total Charges)	

Remark

Market Movement		Mistakes	
Balance B/D		Balance C/D	

Observations

Date			Day			
Segment	Quantity	Buying Price	Selling Price	Target Or Stoploss	Risk/ Reward	Profit/Loss

Total Profit/Loss	
Charges	
Brokerage	
STT	
Other Charges	
Total Charges	
Grand Total (Profit - Total Charges/Loss + Total Charges)	

Remark

Market Movement		Mistakes	
Balance B/D		Balance C/D	

Observations

Trading खाता

Date			Day			
Segment	Quantity	Buying Price	Selling Price	Target Or Stoploss	Risk/ Reward	Profit/Loss

Total Profit/Loss	
Charges	
Brokerage	
STT	
Other Charges	
Total Charges	
Grand Total (Profit - Total Charges/Loss + Total Charges)	

Remark

Market Movement		Mistakes	
Balance B/D		Balance C/D	

Observations

Date			Day			
Segment	Quantity	Buying Price	Selling Price	Target Or Stoploss	Risk/ Reward	Profit/Loss

Total Profit/Loss	
Charges	
Brokerage	
STT	
Other Charges	
Total Charges	
Grand Total (Profit - Total Charges/Loss + Total Charges)	

Remark

Market Movement		Mistakes	
Balance B/D		Balance C/D	

Observations

Trading खाता

Date				Day			
Segment	Quantity	Buying Price	Selling Price	Target Or Stoploss	Risk/ Reward	Profit/Loss

Total Profit/Loss	
Charges	
Brokerage	
STT	
Other Charges	
Total Charges	
Grand Total (Profit - Total Charges/Loss + Total Charges)	

Remark

Market Movement		Mistakes	
Balance B/D		Balance C/D	

Observations

Date			Day			
Segment	Quantity	Buying Price	Selling Price	Target Or Stoploss	Risk/ Reward	Profit/Loss

Total Profit/Loss	
Charges	
Brokerage	
STT	
Other Charges	
Total Charges	
Grand Total (Profit - Total Charges/Loss + Total Charges)	

Remark

Market Movement		Mistakes	
Balance B/D		Balance C/D	

Observations

Trading खाता

Date				Day			
Segment	Quantity	Buying Price	Selling Price	Target Or Stoploss	Risk/ Reward	Profit/Loss
Total Profit/Loss						
Charges						
Brokerage						
STT						
Other Charges						
Total Charges						
Grand Total (Profit - Total Charges/Loss + Total Charges)						

Remark

Market Movement		Mistakes	
Balance B/D		**Balance C/D**	

Observations

Date			Day			
Segment	Quantity	Buying Price	Selling Price	Target Or Stoploss	Risk/ Reward	Profit/Loss

Total Profit/Loss	
Charges	
Brokerage	
STT	
Other Charges	
Total Charges	
Grand Total (Profit - Total Charges/Loss + Total Charges)	

Remark

Market Movement		Mistakes	
Balance B/D		Balance C/D	

Observations

Trading खाता

Date			Day			
Segment	Quantity	Buying Price	Selling Price	Target Or Stoploss	Risk/ Reward	Profit/Loss

Total Profit/Loss	
Charges	
Brokerage	
STT	
Other Charges	
Total Charges	
Grand Total (Profit - Total Charges/Loss + Total Charges)	

Remark

Market Movement		Mistakes	
Balance B/D		Balance C/D	

Observations

Date			Day			
Segment	Quantity	Buying Price	Selling Price	Target Or Stoploss	Risk/ Reward	Profit/Loss

Total Profit/Loss	
Charges	
Brokerage	
STT	
Other Charges	
Total Charges	
Grand Total (Profit - Total Charges/Loss + Total Charges)	

Remark

Market Movement		Mistakes	
Balance B/D		Balance C/D	

Observations

Trading खाता

Date				Day			
Segment	Quantity	Buying Price	Selling Price		Target Or Stoploss	Risk/ Reward	Profit/Loss
Total Profit/Loss							
Charges							
Brokerage							
STT							
Other Charges							
Total Charges							
Grand Total (Profit - Total Charges/Loss + Total Charges)							

Remark

Market Movement		Mistakes	
Balance B/D		**Balance C/D**	

Observations

Date			Day			
Segment	Quantity	Buying Price	Selling Price	Target Or Stoploss	Risk/ Reward	Profit/Loss

Total Profit/Loss	
Charges	
Brokerage	
STT	
Other Charges	
Total Charges	
Grand Total (Profit - Total Charges/Loss + Total Charges)	

Remark

Market Movement		Mistakes	
Balance B/D		Balance C/D	

Observations

Trading खाता

Date			Day			
Segment	Quantity	Buying Price	Selling Price	Target Or Stoploss	Risk/ Reward	Profit/Loss
Total Profit/Loss						
Charges						
Brokerage						
STT						
Other Charges						
Total Charges						
Grand Total (Profit - Total Charges/Loss + Total Charges)						

Remark

Market Movement		Mistakes	
Balance B/D		**Balance C/D**	

Observations

Date			Day			
Segment	Quantity	Buying Price	Selling Price	Target Or Stoploss	Risk/ Reward	Profit/Loss

Total Profit/Loss	
Charges	
Brokerage	
STT	
Other Charges	
Total Charges	
Grand Total (Profit - Total Charges/Loss + Total Charges)	

Remark

Market Movement		Mistakes	
Balance B/D		Balance C/D	

Observations

Trading खाता

Date			Day			
Segment	Quantity	Buying Price	Selling Price	Target Or Stoploss	Risk/ Reward	Profit/Loss
Total Profit/Loss						
Charges						
Brokerage						
STT						
Other Charges						
Total Charges						
Grand Total (Profit - Total Charges/Loss + Total Charges)						

Remark

Market Movement		Mistakes	
Balance B/D		**Balance C/D**	

Observations

Date			Day			
Segment	Quantity	Buying Price	Selling Price	Target Or Stoploss	Risk/ Reward	Profit/Loss

Total Profit/Loss	
Charges	
Brokerage	
STT	
Other Charges	
Total Charges	
Grand Total (Profit - Total Charges/Loss + Total Charges)	

Remark

Market Movement		Mistakes	
Balance B/D		Balance C/D	

Observations

Trading खाता

Date				Day			
Segment	Quantity	Buying Price	Selling Price	Target Or Stoploss	Risk/ Reward	Profit/Loss

Total Profit/Loss	
Charges	
Brokerage	
STT	
Other Charges	
Total Charges	
Grand Total (Profit - Total Charges/Loss + Total Charges)	

Remark

Market Movement		Mistakes	
Balance B/D		**Balance C/D**	

Observations

Date			Day			
Segment	Quantity	Buying Price	Selling Price	Target Or Stoploss	Risk/ Reward	Profit/Loss

Total Profit/Loss	
Charges	
Brokerage	
STT	
Other Charges	
Total Charges	
Grand Total (Profit - Total Charges/Loss + Total Charges)	

Remark

Market Movement		Mistakes	
Balance B/D		Balance C/D	

Observations

Trading खाता

Date			Day			
Segment	Quantity	Buying Price	Selling Price	Target Or Stoploss	Risk/ Reward	Profit/Loss
Total Profit/Loss						
Charges						
Brokerage						
STT						
Other Charges						
Total Charges						
Grand Total (Profit - Total Charges/Loss + Total Charges)						

Remark

Market Movement		Mistakes	
Balance B/D		**Balance C/D**	

Observations

Date			Day			
Segment	Quantity	Buying Price	Selling Price	Target Or Stoploss	Risk/ Reward	Profit/Loss

Total Profit/Loss	
Charges	
Brokerage	
STT	
Other Charges	
Total Charges	
Grand Total (Profit - Total Charges/Loss + Total Charges)	

Remark

Market Movement		Mistakes	
Balance B/D		Balance C/D	

Observations

Trading खाता

Date			Day			
Segment	Quantity	Buying Price	Selling Price	Target Or Stoploss	Risk/ Reward	Profit/Loss

Total Profit/Loss	
Charges	
Brokerage	
STT	
Other Charges	
Total Charges	
Grand Total (Profit - Total Charges/Loss + Total Charges)	

Remark

Market Movement		Mistakes	
Balance B/D		Balance C/D	

Observations

Date			Day			
Segment	Quantity	Buying Price	Selling Price	Target Or Stoploss	Risk/ Reward	Profit/Loss

Total Profit/Loss	
Charges	
Brokerage	
STT	
Other Charges	
Total Charges	
Grand Total (Profit - Total Charges/Loss + Total Charges)	

Remark

Market Movement		Mistakes	
Balance B/D		Balance C/D	

Observations

Trading खाता

Date				Day			
Segment	Quantity	Buying Price	Selling Price	Target Or Stoploss	Risk/ Reward	Profit/Loss	

Total Profit/Loss	
Charges	
Brokerage	
STT	
Other Charges	
Total Charges	
Grand Total (Profit - Total Charges/Loss + Total Charges)	

Remark

Market Movement		Mistakes	
Balance B/D		Balance C/D	

Observations

Date			Day			
Segment	Quantity	Buying Price	Selling Price	Target Or Stoploss	Risk/ Reward	Profit/Loss

Total Profit/Loss	
Charges	
Brokerage	
STT	
Other Charges	
Total Charges	
Grand Total (Profit - Total Charges/Loss + Total Charges)	

Remark

Market Movement		Mistakes	
Balance B/D		Balance C/D	

Observations

Trading खाता

Date			Day			
Segment	Quantity	Buying Price	Selling Price	Target Or Stoploss	Risk/ Reward	Profit/Loss
Total Profit/Loss						
Charges						
Brokerage						
STT						
Other Charges						
Total Charges						
Grand Total (Profit - Total Charges/Loss + Total Charges)						

Remark

Market Movement		Mistakes	
Balance B/D		Balance C/D	

Observations

Date			Day			
Segment	Quantity	Buying Price	Selling Price	Target Or Stoploss	Risk/ Reward	Profit/Loss
Total Profit/Loss						
Charges						
Brokerage						
STT						
Other Charges						
Total Charges						
Grand Total (Profit - Total Charges/Loss + Total Charges)						

Remark

Market Movement		Mistakes	
Balance B/D		Balance C/D	

Observations

Trading खाता

Date				Day			
Segment	Quantity	Buying Price	Selling Price	Target Or Stoploss	Risk/ Reward	Profit/Loss
Total Profit/Loss			
Charges			
Brokerage			
STT			
Other Charges			
Total Charges			
Grand Total (Profit - Total Charges/Loss + Total Charges)			

Remark

Market Movement		Mistakes	
Balance B/D		**Balance C/D**	

Observations

Date			Day			
Segment	Quantity	Buying Price	Selling Price	Target Or Stoploss	Risk/ Reward	Profit/Loss

Total Profit/Loss	
Charges	
Brokerage	
STT	
Other Charges	
Total Charges	
Grand Total (Profit - Total Charges/Loss + Total Charges)	

Remark

Market Movement		Mistakes	
Balance B/D		**Balance C/D**	

Observations

Trading खाता

Date				Day			
Segment	Quantity	Buying Price	Selling Price	Target Or Stoploss		Risk/ Reward	Profit/Loss

Total Profit/Loss	
Charges	
Brokerage	
STT	
Other Charges	
Total Charges	
Grand Total (Profit - Total Charges/Loss + Total Charges)	

Remark

Market Movement		Mistakes	
Balance B/D		**Balance C/D**	

Observations

Date			Day			
Segment	Quantity	Buying Price	Selling Price	Target Or Stoploss	Risk/ Reward	Profit/Loss

Total Profit/Loss	
Charges	
Brokerage	
STT	
Other Charges	
Total Charges	
Grand Total (Profit - Total Charges/Loss + Total Charges)	

Remark

Market Movement		Mistakes	
Balance B/D		Balance C/D	

Observations

Trading खाता

Date				Day			
Segment	Quantity	Buying Price	Selling Price	Target Or Stoploss	Risk/ Reward	Profit/Loss
Total Profit/Loss						
Charges						
Brokerage						
STT						
Other Charges						
Total Charges						
Grand Total (Profit - Total Charges/Loss + Total Charges)						

Remark

Market Movement		Mistakes	
Balance B/D		Balance C/D	

Observations

Date			Day			
Segment	Quantity	Buying Price	Selling Price	Target Or Stoploss	Risk/ Reward	Profit/Loss

Total Profit/Loss	
Charges	
Brokerage	
STT	
Other Charges	
Total Charges	
Grand Total (Profit - Total Charges/Loss + Total Charges)	

Remark

Market Movement		Mistakes	
Balance B/D		Balance C/D	

Observations

Trading खाता

Date			Day			
Segment	Quantity	Buying Price	Selling Price	Target Or Stoploss	Risk/ Reward	Profit/Loss
Total Profit/Loss						
Charges						
Brokerage						
STT						
Other Charges						
Total Charges						
Grand Total (Profit - Total Charges/Loss + Total Charges)						

Remark

Market Movement		Mistakes	
Balance B/D		Balance C/D	

Observations

Date			Day			
Segment	Quantity	Buying Price	Selling Price	Target Or Stoploss	Risk/ Reward	Profit/Loss

Total Profit/Loss	
Charges	
Brokerage	
STT	
Other Charges	
Total Charges	
Grand Total (Profit - Total Charges/Loss + Total Charges)	

Remark

Market Movement		Mistakes	
Balance B/D		Balance C/D	

Observations

Trading खाता

Date				Day			
Segment	Quantity	Buying Price	Selling Price		Target Or Stoploss	Risk/ Reward	Profit/Loss
Total Profit/Loss							
Charges							
Brokerage							
STT							
Other Charges							
Total Charges							
Grand Total (Profit - Total Charges/Loss + Total Charges)							

Remark

Market Movement		Mistakes	
Balance B/D		**Balance C/D**	

Observations

Date			Day			
Segment	Quantity	Buying Price	Selling Price	Target Or Stoploss	Risk/Reward	Profit/Loss

Total Profit/Loss	
Charges	
Brokerage	
STT	
Other Charges	
Total Charges	
Grand Total (Profit - Total Charges/Loss + Total Charges)	

Remark

Market Movement		Mistakes	
Balance B/D		Balance C/D	

Observations

Trading खाता

Date				Day			
Segment	Quantity	Buying Price	Selling Price	Target Or Stoploss	Risk/ Reward	Profit/Loss

Total Profit/Loss	
Charges	
Brokerage	
STT	
Other Charges	
Total Charges	
Grand Total (Profit - Total Charges/Loss + Total Charges)	

Remark

Market Movement		Mistakes	
Balance B/D		Balance C/D	

Observations

Date			Day			
Segment	Quantity	Buying Price	Selling Price	Target Or Stoploss	Risk/ Reward	Profit/Loss

Total Profit/Loss	
Charges	
Brokerage	
STT	
Other Charges	
Total Charges	
Grand Total (Profit - Total Charges/Loss + Total Charges)	

Remark

Market Movement		Mistakes	
Balance B/D		Balance C/D	

Observations

Trading खाता

Date				Day			
Segment	Quantity	Buying Price	Selling Price	Target Or Stoploss	Risk/ Reward	Profit/Loss	
Total Profit/Loss							
Charges							
Brokerage							
STT							
Other Charges							
Total Charges							
Grand Total (Profit - Total Charges/Loss + Total Charges)							

Remark

Market Movement		Mistakes	
Balance B/D		Balance C/D	

Observations

Date			Day			
Segment	Quantity	Buying Price	Selling Price	Target Or Stoploss	Risk/ Reward	Profit/Loss

Total Profit/Loss	
Charges	
Brokerage	
STT	
Other Charges	
Total Charges	
Grand Total (Profit - Total Charges/Loss + Total Charges)	

Remark

Market Movement		Mistakes	
Balance B/D		Balance C/D	

Observations

Trading खाता

Date				Day		
Segment	Quantity	Buying Price	Selling Price	Target Or Stoploss	Risk/ Reward	Profit/Loss

Total Profit/Loss	
Charges	
Brokerage	
STT	
Other Charges	
Total Charges	
Grand Total (Profit - Total Charges/Loss + Total Charges)	

Remark

Market Movement		Mistakes	
Balance B/D		Balance C/D	

Observations

Date			Day			
Segment	Quantity	Buying Price	Selling Price	Target Or Stoploss	Risk/ Reward	Profit/Loss
Total Profit/Loss						
Charges						
Brokerage						
STT						
Other Charges						
Total Charges						
Grand Total (Profit - Total Charges/Loss + Total Charges)						

Remark

Market Movement		Mistakes	
Balance B/D		**Balance C/D**	

Observations

Trading खाता

Date				Day			
Segment	Quantity	Buying Price	Selling Price	Target Or Stoploss		Risk/ Reward	Profit/Loss
Total Profit/Loss							
Charges							
Brokerage							
STT							
Other Charges							
Total Charges							
Grand Total (Profit - Total Charges/Loss + Total Charges)							

Remark

Market Movement		Mistakes	
Balance B/D		Balance C/D	

Observations

Date				Day			
Segment	Quantity	Buying Price	Selling Price	Target Or Stoploss		Risk/ Reward	Profit/Loss

Total Profit/Loss	
Charges	
Brokerage	
STT	
Other Charges	
Total Charges	
Grand Total (Profit - Total Charges/Loss + Total Charges)	

Remark

Market Movement		Mistakes	
Balance B/D		Balance C/D	

Observations

Trading खाता

Date			Day			
Segment	Quantity	Buying Price	Selling Price	Target Or Stoploss	Risk/ Reward	Profit/Loss

Total Profit/Loss	
Charges	
Brokerage	
STT	
Other Charges	
Total Charges	
Grand Total (Profit - Total Charges/Loss + Total Charges)	

Remark

Market Movement		Mistakes	
Balance B/D		Balance C/D	

Observations

Date			Day			
Segment	Quantity	Buying Price	Selling Price	Target Or Stoploss	Risk/ Reward	Profit/Loss

Total Profit/Loss	
Charges	
Brokerage	
STT	
Other Charges	
Total Charges	
Grand Total (Profit - Total Charges/Loss + Total Charges)	

Remark

Market Movement		Mistakes	
Balance B/D		Balance C/D	

Observations

Trading खाता

Date				Day			
Segment	Quantity	Buying Price	Selling Price	Target Or Stoploss	Risk/ Reward	Profit/Loss

Total Profit/Loss	
Charges	
Brokerage	
STT	
Other Charges	
Total Charges	
Grand Total (Profit - Total Charges/Loss + Total Charges)	

Remark

Market Movement		Mistakes	
Balance B/D		**Balance C/D**	

Observations

Date			Day			
Segment	Quantity	Buying Price	Selling Price	Target Or Stoploss	Risk/ Reward	Profit/Loss
Total Profit/Loss						
Charges						
Brokerage						
STT						
Other Charges						
Total Charges						
Grand Total (Profit - Total Charges/Loss + Total Charges)						

Remark

Market Movement		Mistakes	
Balance B/D		Balance C/D	

Observations

Trading खाता

Date			Day			
Segment	Quantity	Buying Price	Selling Price	Target Or Stoploss	Risk/ Reward	Profit/Loss
Total Profit/Loss						
Charges						
Brokerage						
STT						
Other Charges						
Total Charges						
Grand Total (Profit - Total Charges/Loss + Total Charges)						

Remark

Market Movement		Mistakes	
Balance B/D		**Balance C/D**	

Observations

Date			Day			
Segment	Quantity	Buying Price	Selling Price	Target Or Stoploss	Risk/ Reward	Profit/Loss

Total Profit/Loss	
Charges	
Brokerage	
STT	
Other Charges	
Total Charges	
Grand Total (Profit - Total Charges/Loss + Total Charges)	

Remark

Market Movement		Mistakes	
Balance B/D		Balance C/D	

Observations

Trading खाता

Date				Day			
Segment	Quantity	Buying Price	Selling Price	Target Or Stoploss	Risk/ Reward	Profit/Loss	
Total Profit/Loss							
Charges							
Brokerage							
STT							
Other Charges							
Total Charges							
Grand Total (Profit - Total Charges/Loss + Total Charges)							

Remark

Market Movement		Mistakes	
Balance B/D		Balance C/D	

Observations

Date			Day			
Segment	Quantity	Buying Price	Selling Price	Target Or Stoploss	Risk/ Reward	Profit/Loss

Total Profit/Loss	
Charges	
Brokerage	
STT	
Other Charges	
Total Charges	
Grand Total (Profit - Total Charges/Loss + Total Charges)	

Remark

Market Movement		Mistakes	
Balance B/D		Balance C/D	

Observations

Trading खाता

Date				Day			
Segment	Quantity	Buying Price	Selling Price	Target Or Stoploss		Risk/ Reward	Profit/Loss

Total Profit/Loss	
Charges	
Brokerage	
STT	
Other Charges	
Total Charges	
Grand Total (Profit - Total Charges/Loss + Total Charges)	

Remark

Market Movement		Mistakes	
Balance B/D		Balance C/D	

Observations

Date			Day			
Segment	Quantity	Buying Price	Selling Price	Target Or Stoploss	Risk/ Reward	Profit/Loss

Total Profit/Loss	
Charges	
Brokerage	
STT	
Other Charges	
Total Charges	
Grand Total (Profit - Total Charges/Loss + Total Charges)	

Remark

Market Movement		Mistakes	
Balance B/D		Balance C/D	

Observations

Trading खाता

Date				Day			
Segment	Quantity	Buying Price	Selling Price	Target Or Stoploss	Risk/ Reward	Profit/Loss

Total Profit/Loss	
Charges	
Brokerage	
STT	
Other Charges	
Total Charges	
Grand Total (Profit - Total Charges/Loss + Total Charges)	

Remark

Market Movement		Mistakes	
Balance B/D		**Balance C/D**	

Observations

Date			Day			
Segment	Quantity	Buying Price	Selling Price	Target Or Stoploss	Risk/ Reward	Profit/Loss

Total Profit/Loss	
Charges	
Brokerage	
STT	
Other Charges	
Total Charges	
Grand Total (Profit - Total Charges/Loss + Total Charges)	

Remark

Market Movement		Mistakes	
Balance B/D		Balance C/D	

Observations

Trading खाता

Date			Day			
Segment	Quantity	Buying Price	Selling Price	Target Or Stoploss	Risk/ Reward	Profit/Loss
Total Profit/Loss						
Charges						
Brokerage						
STT						
Other Charges						
Total Charges						
Grand Total (Profit - Total Charges/Loss + Total Charges)						

Remark

Market Movement		Mistakes	
Balance B/D		Balance C/D	

Observations

Date			Day			
Segment	Quantity	Buying Price	Selling Price	Target Or Stoploss	Risk/ Reward	Profit/Loss

Total Profit/Loss	
Charges	
Brokerage	
STT	
Other Charges	
Total Charges	
Grand Total (Profit - Total Charges/Loss + Total Charges)	

Remark

Market Movement		Mistakes	
Balance B/D		Balance C/D	

Observations

Trading खाता

Date				Day			
Segment	Quantity	Buying Price	Selling Price	Target Or Stoploss	Risk/ Reward	Profit/Loss	

Total Profit/Loss	
Charges	
Brokerage	
STT	
Other Charges	
Total Charges	
Grand Total (Profit - Total Charges/Loss + Total Charges)	

Remark

Market Movement		Mistakes	
Balance B/D		Balance C/D	

Observations

Date			Day			
Segment	Quantity	Buying Price	Selling Price	Target Or Stoploss	Risk/ Reward	Profit/Loss

Total Profit/Loss	
Charges	
Brokerage	
STT	
Other Charges	
Total Charges	
Grand Total (Profit - Total Charges/Loss + Total Charges)	

Remark

Market Movement		Mistakes	
Balance B/D		Balance C/D	

Observations

Trading खाता

Date			Day			
Segment	Quantity	Buying Price	Selling Price	Target Or Stoploss	Risk/ Reward	Profit/Loss

Total Profit/Loss	
Charges	
Brokerage	
STT	
Other Charges	
Total Charges	
Grand Total (Profit - Total Charges/Loss + Total Charges)	

Remark

Market Movement		Mistakes	
Balance B/D		**Balance C/D**	

Observations

Date			Day			
Segment	Quantity	Buying Price	Selling Price	Target Or Stoploss	Risk/ Reward	Profit/Loss

Total Profit/Loss	
Charges	
Brokerage	
STT	
Other Charges	
Total Charges	
Grand Total (Profit - Total Charges/Loss + Total Charges)	

Remark

Market Movement		Mistakes	
Balance B/D		Balance C/D	

Observations

Trading खाता

Date				Day			
Segment	Quantity	Buying Price	Selling Price	Target Or Stoploss		Risk/ Reward	Profit/Loss
Total Profit/Loss							
Charges							
Brokerage							
STT							
Other Charges							
Total Charges							
Grand Total (Profit - Total Charges/Loss + Total Charges)							

Remark

Market Movement		Mistakes	
Balance B/D		**Balance C/D**	

Observations

Date			Day			
Segment	Quantity	Buying Price	Selling Price	Target Or Stoploss	Risk/Reward	Profit/Loss

Total Profit/Loss	
Charges	
Brokerage	
STT	
Other Charges	
Total Charges	
Grand Total (Profit - Total Charges/Loss + Total Charges)	

Remark

Market Movement		Mistakes	
Balance B/D		**Balance C/D**	

Observations

Trading खाता

Date			Day			
Segment	Quantity	Buying Price	Selling Price	Target Or Stoploss	Risk/ Reward	Profit/Loss

Total Profit/Loss	
Charges	
Brokerage	
STT	
Other Charges	
Total Charges	
Grand Total (Profit - Total Charges/Loss + Total Charges)	

Remark

Market Movement		Mistakes	
Balance B/D		Balance C/D	

Observations

Date			Day			
Segment	Quantity	Buying Price	Selling Price	Target Or Stoploss	Risk/ Reward	Profit/Loss
Total Profit/Loss						
Charges						
Brokerage						
STT						
Other Charges						
Total Charges						
Grand Total (Profit - Total Charges/Loss + Total Charges)						

Remark

Market Movement		Mistakes	
Balance B/D		**Balance C/D**	

Observations

Trading खाता

Date				Day			
Segment	Quantity	Buying Price	Selling Price	Target Or Stoploss		Risk/ Reward	Profit/Loss

Total Profit/Loss	
Charges	
Brokerage	
STT	
Other Charges	
Total Charges	
Grand Total (Profit - Total Charges/Loss + Total Charges)	

Remark

Market Movement		Mistakes	
Balance B/D		Balance C/D	

Observations

Date				Day			
Segment	Quantity	Buying Price	Selling Price	Target Or Stoploss		Risk/ Reward	Profit/Loss
Total Profit/Loss							
Charges							
Brokerage							
STT							
Other Charges							
Total Charges							
Grand Total (Profit - Total Charges/Loss + Total Charges)							

Remark

Market Movement		Mistakes	
Balance B/D		Balance C/D	

Observations

I hope after completing 100 trading days challenge your trading changed a lot.

www.ingramcontent.com/pod-product-compliance
Lightning Source LLC
LaVergne TN
LVHW041942070526
838199LV00051BA/2880